THE
IMPRESSIONIST
GARDEN

THE
IMPRESSIONIST
GARDEN

*Ideas and Inspiration from the Gardens
and Paintings of the Impressionists*

DEREK FELL

CAROL SOUTHERN BOOKS · NEW YORK

For my wife, Carolyn

"Ah, what portraits could be made from nature with photography and painting" VAN GOGH

The Impressionist Garden
Copyright © Frances Lincoln Limited 1994
Text copyright © 1994 Derek Fell
All photographs copyright © Derek Fell 1994 except those listed on page 144.The copyright in the photographs is the property of the photographers unless otherwise stated.

Published by Carol Southern Books, an imprint of Crown Publishers, Inc, 201 East 50th Street, New York, New York 10022.
Member of the Crown Publishing Group.

Random House, Inc. New York, Toronto, London, Sydney, Auckland

Carol Southern Books and colophon are trademarks of Crown Publishers, Inc.

First published in Great Britain in 1994 by
Frances Lincoln Limited
4 Torriano Mews, Torriano Avenue
London NW5 2RZ

Manufactured in Hong Kong

Library of Congress Cataloging-in-Publication Data

Fell, Derek
    The Impressionist Garden: ideas and inspiration from the gardens and paintings of the impressionists / Derek Fell. — 1st Frances Lincoln ed.
        p. cm.
    Includes bibliographical references (p.140) and index.
    1. Landscape gardening. 2. Gardens — Designs and plans.
3. Gardens — Pictorial works. 4. Gardens in art. 5. Impressionist artists — Homes and haunts. 6. Impressionism (Art). I. Title.
SB473.I4452 1994
712—dc20   93–42029
                                                      CIP

ISBN 0-517-59851-5
10 9 8 7 6 5 4 3 2 1
First Edition

ABOVE Rosa *'Painter Renoir', named after the artist, still grows in his garden, Les Collettes, in the south of France.*

OPPOSITE Caillebotte was as enthusiastic and dedicated a gardener as Monet. Roses – Garden at Petit-Gennevilliers (c.1886), one of many paintings he did of his own large garden, shows what appear to be the recently introduced roses 'La France' and 'American Beauty'.*

PAGE ONE A tender blue potato vine (Solanum rantonnetii) cascades from one of Monet's blue and white Oriental pots on the wooden porch that runs behind his house at Giverny.*

PREVIOUS PAGES Van Gogh's painting Flower Garden with Path (1888) inspired the author to plant a cutting garden at his estate, Cedaridge Farm, using flowers in similar colors.*

CONTENTS

The Impressionists' Love of Gardens

The great French Impressionists – painters such as Monet, Renoir, Pissarro, their immediate successors Cézanne and Van Gogh, and American Impressionists such as Frieseke and Hassam not only revolutionized the art of painting, they also introduced innovative ways of looking at gardens. The new vision that they brought to their art was reflected in their gardens, both on canvas and in reality. It is by studying the gardens – many of which survive – as well as the potent images that the painters made, that it becomes possible to reinterpret their vision in gardens today.

The Impressionists' paintings of gardens were never intended to be botanically or architecturally accurate. Indeed, art historians and horticulturists today disagree about the particular plants and structural details depicted, but the paintings do convey the artists' interpretation of their gardens and express their joyous response to color, the play of light, the vibrancy of leaves and flowers, water reflections, and the sensations of shimmer on a sunny day or mist on a wintry morning.

The obvious pleasure that they took in life out of doors is apparent in the number of paintings of natural landscapes, cityscapes, seascapes and gardens. Renoir even went to the trouble of building a studio in his garden with glass walls on two sides so he could paint his olive orchard while protecting his frail health from too much sun or sudden chills; his life-long friend Monet constructed a special studio boat so that he could more faithfully capture the many moods of water.

Impressionism is closely associated with painting *en plein air*; however, although the Impressionists were not the first group of painters to work outside, what was revolutionary was their commitment to capture and record the fleeting moment, especially in the open air. Also new was the way they applied the paint to canvas – often with flickering brushstrokes using different colors in juxtaposition – and the way they abandoned conventional methods of modelling form by using color rather than sharply outlined shapes or strong contrasts of light and shade. Equally new, and more controversial at the time, was their choice of subject matter – their portrayal of intimate details of city and country life. Even their landscapes were neither heroic (like Turner's) nor idyllic (like many of Corot's), but were simply what attracted their attention beyond their windows or on a stroll during a day trip. By the same token, the gardens they depicted were mostly domestic.

The artistic roots of Impressionism lead back through its immediate precursors – the painters of the Barbizon school, Corot, and Courbet. Literature, philosophy, science, political stability and increasing industrialization also played a part in the milieu from which it sprang. Two

Manet's canvas The Monet Family in the Garden (1873) shows Monet tending his garden while his first wife, Camille, and her son Jean enjoy a shady corner of the property that Monet rented at Argenteuil, north-west of Paris. Although planted with commonplace red pelargoniums and over-run with chickens, the garden is presented as an invitingly peaceful place in which to spend an afternoon. While Manet painted, Renoir arrived and, captivated by the shadow patterns, painted a similar scene. Later in the day Monet stopped gardening, took up his brushes, and portrayed Manet at his easel. Monet was to add the Renoir study to his own collection of Impressionist paintings, but the Monet picture of Manet unfortunately no longer survives.

practical inventions encouraged its development: the manufacture of oil paints in tubes made it easier to paint *en plein air*, and – ironically – the development of the portable 'snapshot' camera enabled the fleeting moment to be recorded (and used as a reference). The startlingly realistic images of photography also revealed interesting perspectives and unusual viewpoints for innovative compositions.

At the same time and more importantly for the history of gardens, fresh inspiration came from the other side of the world. After Japan opened its borders to world trade, colorful Japanese woodblock prints began to arrive in European capitals. These prints depicted scenes from everyday life – a woman brushing her hair, for example, a close-up view of a flower, a corner of a garden in winter – with a gravitas entirely new to the West. This exotic 'Japonisme' challenged the Impressionists. Van Gogh and Monet in particular acquired valuable collections of Japanese art, and Japanese plants and garden design concepts were to have a strong influence on Monet's garden.

It is significant, too, that the emergence of Impressionism coincided with an explosion of interest in horticulture (the era is now referred to by historians as 'the Golden Age of Horticulture'), when more new plants were introduced into cultivation than at any other time. A period of industrial prosperity had led to a boom in suburban building and more leisure time for the middle classes; concomitant was the increased interest in gardening, stimulated by a flood of new periodicals and nursery catalogs, and the development of commercial greenhouses; the invention of the rubber hose made watering easier, while rotary lawnmowers allowed gardens to feature beautiful expanses of neatly trimmed grass.

Most of the great Impressionist painters had gardens, and these reflected both the personality of the artists and the extent of their horticultural interest. Caillebotte and Monet, men of energy and exacting standards who cultivated their own sizable, complex and highly organized gardens, were fanatical about gardening; they visited horticultural shows and botanical gardens, as well as the test gardens of plant breeders in order to be the first to try a new variety. Renoir, Cézanne and Pissarro took a more *laissez-faire* approach; they saw beauty in old trees, modest vegetable plots and unmowed grasses. Though Van Gogh never experienced the pleasures of owning a garden, he was deeply interested in gardening and wrote long letters to his younger sister Wilhelmina, who had cultivated a garden in Holland, describing color schemes he wanted her to try, and actually naming the plants she should use. While he could not project his personality on to a garden, his state of mind can be traced in his paintings of gardens – bright and cheerful when he was happy or dark and full of foreboding during bouts of melancholy.

As the Impressionists' gardens and paintings are studied, certain themes dominate or recur. The artists used plants as they used paints: to manipulate color effects and to introduce new color schemes – by using hues that intensified by contrast with one another, or that blended and harmonized with each other; they created a shimmering sensation by choosing plants with foamy or lacy white flowers; and took color and interest to the edges of their vision by using trees, tall plants and climbers on supports. On a more down-to-earth level there is a

Monet Painting in his Garden at Argenteuil (1873) by Renoir shows Monet at his easel, with a bed of tall roses in a haphazard planting behind the fence, in the garden he cultivated from 1871 to 1878. Monet's own numerous views of the garden (see pages 68 and 118) show it in a more flattering light with no reference to the proximity of other houses. They all, however, show plantings that were typical of contemporary suburban gardens, making much use of massed bedding plants – the kind of schemes that Monet would almost completely abandon when he came to plant his own garden at Giverny in the 1880s.

similarity between the firm geometric layout of Monet's flower garden at Giverny and Caillebotte's garden at Petit-Gennevilliers; and while Monet trained roses over arches and arbors, Caillebotte trained fruit trees into traditional formal shapes to satisfy his liking for pronounced lines of perspective. Most of the painters raised fruit and vegetables as well as flowers for cutting to use as still lifes, and they all shared a love of wildflowers and woodland and especially of flowering trees.

In our gardens today, it is possible to copy particular garden features, such as Monet's romantic wisteria-canopied bridge, or Van Gogh's stunning combination of blue irises with orange calendulas, and also to adapt the less tangible ideas more freely. In my own garden, Cedaridge

In Orange Trees *(1878), Caillebotte makes a pair of Versailles tubs seem larger than life by cutting the citrus foliage off the top of his canvas, and contrasting the solid, chunky shapes of the planters with the filigree wrought-iron of a table and cluster of ornate seats. Painted at his family estate at Yerres, south of Paris, the scene of tranquil domesticity conveys the formality of the garden. A sweeping arch of gravel leads the eye from deep shade into bright sunlight where a conventionally circular flower bed is filled with bedding plants. Versailles tubs were popular garden features at the time and appear in other Impressionist paintings, including works by Monet and Van Gogh. Similar classic planters, metalwork furniture and the green slatted bench are all commercially available today.*

Farm, Pennsylvania, for example, one area emulates a Provençal cutting garden painted by Van Gogh; a small pond and stream is a scaled-down version of Monet's water garden, complete with waterlilies and bridge; there are leaf tunnels like those in Cézanne's garden today, and meadow plantings evoke the cliff-top paintings of Hassam, while copies of Renoir's rope swing, Pissarro's wooden wheelbarrow, Manet's bench and Caillebotte's garden gate provide decorative accents.

By describing the gardens and analysing the paintings, this book aims to make the Impressionist garden aesthetic accessible to gardeners today. With the help of photographs of gardens which have been inspired by the Impressionist masters, and with practical planting plans, it explains how the ideas seen in Impressionist gardens can be adapted to a modern setting and a smaller compass.

Berthe Morisot, who married Manet's brother Eugène, often painted intimate family scenes such as Catching Butterflies *(1874). Here, children pause while chasing butterflies in what was known as a* jardin anglais, *an informal garden of trees, shrubs and grass. The loose brushstrokes add a feeling of spontaneity to the scene and also emphasize the informal, almost wild, quality of the garden.*

THE IMPRESSIONISTS' GARDENS TODAY

In a world that has changed drastically this century through two World Wars, population explosions, and industrial and suburban blight, it is surprising to find that many of the gardens that the Impressionists planted – and many more that they painted – survive today, either as a result of restoration, or because they remained in private hands with owners who valued their historic associations. The gardens owned by Monet, Renoir and Cézanne are well preserved, maintained as museums, with the houses and gardens intact; Caillebotte's family estate at Yerres is now a municipal park, but part of the walled kitchen garden is still planted with rows of vegetables exactly as Caillebotte painted them. Caillebotte's own garden at Petit-Gennevilliers, however, is long gone – a victim of industrial development. Many of the gardens that Van Gogh painted in Provence still exist: the asylum at Saint-Rémy remains much as it did in his day, with a well-marked trail to the places he painted beyond the asylum walls; the hospital garden at Arles survives, as do many of the gardens and landscapes Van Gogh painted at Auvers, near Paris.

Of all the Impressionists' gardens that exist today, Giverny is the most celebrated and the most visited garden in the world. Monet lived there for half his life; he devoted much of his prodigious energy to it, replanting, extending and improving it. Unlike most other gardens, it was created not just as a garden to enjoy, but as one to be painted. Indeed, it is the subject of over five hundred of Monet's works. It is built up in a myriad "brush strokes" of shimmering color and seen through half-closed eyes instantly becomes recognizable as an Impressionist painting. No wonder that Monet described it as his greatest work of art.

Monet moved to Giverny – a farming community north of Paris – in 1883, when he was looking for somewhere to settle with his family. At first he rented the large pink house and its spacious walled garden that contained mostly fruit trees and hedges of boxwood, but as his paintings began to sell steadily he was able to purchase the property seven years later, maintaining it as his home until his death in 1926. Initially Monet did the planting and his children and step-children helped with watering and weeding, but by 1892 Monet was employing a head gardener and five assistant gardeners. In the 1890s he was able to purchase some more, adjacent land to make a water garden, so enlarging the property to over four acres.

Monet was not only fortunate in the prevailing climate of Normandy, which has summer rainfall similar to that in the south of England, but also in the deep alluvial soils of Giverny, which stands on the flood plain of the River Seine. He appreciated the value of good garden compost as a soil conditioner and natural garden fertilizer: he brought in cartloads of manure and peat that increased the soil depth of all the flower beds

MONET'S GARDEN AT GIVERNY
1 Main house and first studio
2 Livestock pens
3 Third studio (The Waterlily Studio)
4 Gardener's cottage
5 Flower beds, 'sunrise' borders
6 Gravel exhedra and Monet's curved benches
7 Lower entrance
8 Grande Allée
9 Tunnel from Clos Normand to water garden
10 Plant nursery
11 Flower beds, 'sunset' borders
12 Greenhouse and cold frames
13 Second studio
14 Top entrance and wall espaliered with pear trees
15 Entrance to water garden
16 Japanese bridge
17 Waterlily pond
18 Smaller bridges
19 Boat dock and rose arches
20 Bamboo grove
21 Stroll path

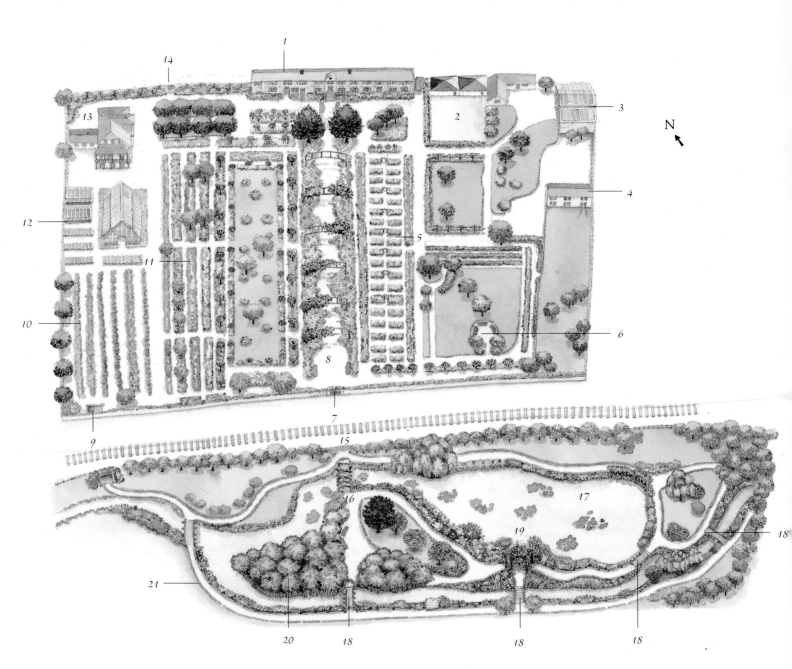

and he bordered them with bricks or stones. The fashion for mounding each bed up to a height of 60 centimetres (2 feet) in the middle, allowed plants to be displayed in tiers, and also facilitated drainage.

The walled flower garden is known as the Clos Normand. It is bisected by the Grande Allée, a broad gravel path that leads from the main door of the house to wide green gates at the bottom of the garden. Parallel flower beds, each 2 metres (7 feet) wide, line the walk, while six green painted metal arches supporting climbing roses form a floral tunnel overhead.

On either side of the Grande Allée are a series of rectangular beds. To the east they are set out in two parallel rows of small beds; to the west longer narrower beds run from north to south. The view from Monet's bedroom in winter shows a highly formal design of ruler-straight edges, but for most of the year the lines seem to dissolve under a profusion of flowers. One visiting French journalist described the garden in 1904 as "... divided into tidy 'squares' like any market garden ... substitute flowers for carrots and lettuce, in rows just as close together, and you can work wonders – if you know how to play the floral keyboard and are a great colorist. It is this profusion – this teeming aspect that gives the garden a special quality."

A pair of flowering Japanese crab apple trees (Malus floribunda) in front of the façade of the house at Giverny provide a canopy of delicate white blossom in the spring. They are among the first trees that Monet planted, to replace some tired fruit trees. The twisting trunks now resemble some of the dramatic shapes made by weather-worn trees painted by Monet along the Normandy coast and Côte d'Azur.

The beds are intensively planted, some sporting all colors of the rainbow; others more faithful to Monet's original color plans, especially blue and yellow, orange and yellow, and pink and blue. They are punctuated with flowering shrubs and trees, including a beautiful silk tree *(Albizia julibrissin)* that has layered branches and small mimosa-like yellow-green leaflets. A bonus in summer is its rosy-pink flowers shaped like upturned bristle brushes. The outstretched branches and the pattern of multiple leaflets cast shadow patterns delicate enough to allow flowering plants to grow right up to its trunk. Standard roses, obtained by grafting a shrub rose onto a straight rose stem, are a special feature of this section; their top-knots of leaves and flowers are trained over a metal umbrella to create a weeping effect.

Though Monet was secretive about his methods, and his garden notes no longer survive, we have a clear idea of what his Giverny garden looked like from his numerous paintings of it, contemporary reports from visitors, and also from a considerable number of photographs taken by himself and his friends. One of the most vivid accounts we have is by Monet's step-son, Jean-Pierre Hoschedé, who grew up at Giverny and described the garden he remembered as a child: "... bit by bit, Monet enlarged his garden, or rather he modified and harmonized it with great simplicity, and in marvellous taste. After dealing with that part of the garden surrounding the house, he turned his attention to the orchard. The west side became a lawn, laid out in the English style, constantly watered and regularly cut. At various points in this lawn Monet planted groups of irises and Oriental poppies. The fruit trees which had died or been grubbed up were replaced, but on a smaller scale, by flowering trees, wild cherries and Japanese crab apple trees. The borders were arranged in various successive steps, each one stocked with different plants; gladioli, larkspur, phlox, asters, large marguerites etc. Overhanging them were supports on which grew climbing clematis of the *montana rubens* type. Practically all the flower beds were surrounded by irises of every possible variety, for Monet had a special liking for this flower. Every year the number of varieties [of other flowers] in his garden was increased, so that there was a large diversity of colors. On the whole

Pink and mauve predominate in Monet's flower garden at Giverny in early June, when mauve and bi-colored purple-and-white bearded irises, pink dame's rocket (Hesperis matronalis), pink peonies and pink rambler roses trained as standards come into bloom. Spires of white foxtail lilies (Eremurus), and drifts of white peonies and white irises in the flower beds beyond help to create the misty, shimmering sensation so beloved by Monet. The effect of waves of color is produced by plants being placed strategically in a series of parallel, long narrow rectangular beds.

AN ARBOR INSPIRED BY MONET'S
GRANDE ALLÉE
*Using one of Monet's favorite color
harmonies, this scheme also includes
many plants that will help to give a
shimmering sensation. Earlier in the
season the color harmony could be
established with pink and white tulips,
hyacinths, forget-me-nots and bleeding
hearts. Later in the year it could be
maintained with Japanese anemones,
dahlias, asters and* Boltonia.

1   Rosa *'America'*
2   Eremurus
3   *White delphiniums*
4   Cleome hassleriana
5   Cosmos *'Daydream'*
6   Paeonia lactiflora *(pink)*
7   Gypsophila paniculata
8   Lavandula angustifolia *'Rosea'*
9   Dianthus chinensis *'Snow Fire'*
10 Lavatera *'Pink Beauty'*
11 Centranthus ruber
12 Clematis *'Hagley Hybrid'*

13 Gaura lindheimeri
14 Paeonia lactiflora *(white)*
15 Lobularia maritima *Summer
    Pastels*
16 Ageratum *'Pinky'*
17 Celosia *'Pink Castle'*
18 Paeonia lactiflora *'Sarah
    Bernhardt'*
19 Cosmos *'Candy Stripe'*
20 Nicotiana alata
21 Cimicifuga racemosa
22 Ipomoea *'Scarlet Star'*

these plants were of the single-petalled type for Monet did not like double ones. At the same time, annual plants were placed among the perennials in such a way that there was always a showing of flowers, and it was almost impossible to see any bare earth."

As Monet settled in at Giverny, he became extremely knowledgeable about planting, learning a great deal from other garden experts, from visits to nurseries and from a large collection of garden books and gardening magazines. Among other flowers that Monet is known to have grown are blue salvia, white and yellow agrimony, stocks, Japanese anemones, monkshood, blue plumbago, morning glories, passion flower, foxgloves, sweetpeas, Asiatic lilies and penstemons which were described by Georges Truffaut, the distinguished gardening expert and long-standing friend of Monet as "the distinctive flower of Claude Monet's garden". As Hoschedé said, "... Monet knew exactly what he wanted from the plants he had bought and planted in specific places. In fact he knew well in advance that when they were in full flower they would have a certain relationship with their adjoining plants, and with the garden as a whole. In this way he achieved exactly the effects he intended, rather as he painted a picture, but in this case not with colors taken from his palette, but with flowers judiciously chosen for their individual colors, mixing them or isolating them in clumps, the whole marvellously planned."

Monet, who kept a very fine table, loved fresh fruit and vegetables, but did not care to mix food crops with flowers. He acquired a separate property, The Blue House, at the other end of the village, where he grew

The Blue House, in the village of Giverny, was purchased by Monet so that he could grow fruit and vegetables in its 2½-acre garden. It is painted the same blue as in Monet's painting, The Blue House, Zaandam (1871), and survives as a private residence. The bushy single-flowered pink rose, R. complicata, would have been available in Monet's time. Borders of pink carnations, pink valerian and blue campanula help to make a striking scheme.

a large assortment of fruit, vegetables and herbs in tidy, geometric-shaped plots. Some cordon-style fruit trees still bear fruit in a section of the garden which is now mostly devoted to lawn and flowers.

Today, under the administration of the Monet Foundation, the main garden is once again a vibrant showpiece, having suffered many years of neglect. Monet's youngest son, Michel, who inherited the property, sadly allowed it to lapse into ruin. However, on Michel's death in 1966, when the house and garden were willed to the State, an aggressive fundraising effort produced enough money to restore the house and then the garden. Giverny is now self-sufficient from admissions, and brings pleasure to many thousands of visitors each year.

Monet's life-long friend Renoir also became deeply attached to his own garden, and was often to use it as a subject for his paintings too, but his attitude towards gardening was almost the antithesis of Monet's. Whereas Monet strove for highly orchestrated effects, which needed constant control and frequent replanting, Renoir preferred to let nature

BELOW Even when his hands and feet became crippled with rheumatism, Renoir continued to paint out of doors in the south of France. He frequently painted in his garden at Les Collettes, where he received visits from other artists including Monet, Modigliani, Matisse and Rodin. When Rodin asked Madame Renoir what her husband's favorite flowers were, she replied, "There are no rare flowers here, but marguerites next to the mimosa. My husband likes common or garden flowers."

have a far freer hand, reproaching the gardeners for pruning too hard or weeding too thoroughly.

Although he had been living in Cagnes-sur-Mer, a fishing village in the south of France, since the late 1890s, it was not until 1907 that Renoir bought Les Collettes, a working farm, in order to save the ancient olive grove from being uprooted to make room for development. At first Renoir had no thought of making a home there, but with his wife Aline's encouragement, a new house, with spectacular views of the Mediterranean Sea (now mostly obscured by tall trees), was built on a rise of ground in a corner of the estate, and the old farmhouse was preserved as a landscape feature. Aline cultivated a citrus and rose garden below a terrace of the new house, for Renoir had a special fondness for roses; he said that painting them helped him to capture the skin tones of women and children. This was the only part of the garden that Renoir allowed to be formal; much of the property was devoted to growing vegetables and fruit – especially citrus fruit – which were sold locally to

BELOW LEFT In House at Cagnes *(1914), Renoir framed the farmhouse at Les Collettes with the sinuous branches of ancient olive trees. A similar view today (BELOW) shows how little has changed. The olive trees – some estimated to be over 500 years old, a strawberry tree (Arbutus unedo) and a lime or linden (Tilia platyphyllos) still cast fascinating shadow patterns over the cobblestone courtyard. Steps on the right lead past a raised bed of irises and pink and red ivy-leaved trailing pelargoniums. The slatted bench is almost exactly the same as that seen in Monet's painting of his garden at Argenteuil on page 118.*

make the estate a self-sufficient smallholding, and Renoir encouraged wild oat grasses, poppies and lavender to seed themselves freely between the widely spaced trees. A friend of Renoir, Georges Rivière, described the slopes of Les Collettes as being "covered with a variety of perfumed trees; and a mass of undergrowth of every shade carpets the earth". Today the planting includes Canary Island date palms, oleander, yucca and agave, while bougainvillea, *Brugmansia* (also known as daturas), agapanthus and arum (calla) lilies help to give a sub-tropical atmosphere to the garden in summer.

On his death in 1919, Renoir left the house and the garden to his youngest son, Coco, who was only eighteen years old at the time. When Coco died in 1969, the property was acquired by the City of Cagnes as a museum. Most of the buildings and garden today are much the same as when Renoir and his family lived there; the original farmhouse appears untouched, though Renoir's outdoor studio has fallen into disrepair. Renoir's bronze *Venus Victrix* is on display, as are several other fine pieces of sculpture and ten original oil paintings.

Both Renoir and Monet were friends of Cézanne, who for a while devoted his time between living in Paris and living with his wealthy parents at their estate, the Jas de Bouffan, in Aix-en-Provence. Following the death of his parents, the family house was sold in 1899, and in 1901 Cézanne purchased a steeply sloping piece of land on the road to Les Lauves, north of Aix, with a fine view of the cathedral. Here he built a

RENOIR'S GARDEN AT LES COLLETTES
(OPPOSITE)

1   *Top entrance*
2   *Blue and lavender bearded iris*
3   *Pittosporum hedge*
4   *Main house*
5   *Fuchsias and daturas*
6   *Strawberry and olive trees underplanted with ivy-leaf geraniums*
7   *Climbing roses*
8   *Venus Victrix sculpture*
9   *Linden tree*
10 *Orange trees underplanted with agapanthus*
11 *Balustrade*
12 *Citrus trees underplanted with roses and lavender*
13 *Lower entrance*
14 *Canary Island date palm*
15 *Dry slope with succulents, oleanders and New Zealand flaxes*
16 *Terraced meadow*
17 *Citrus orchard*
18 *Grape vines*
19 *Vegetable garden*
20 *Farmhouse*
21 *Olive trees*
22 *Fish ponds*

LEFT *The bronze sculpture* Venus Victrix *was designed by Renoir for his garden. It originally stood on a brick pedestal in his wife's formal rose garden. Today the sculpture looks along a wide terrace below Renoir's bedroom. Behind is a bed planted with citrus trees and agapanthus.*

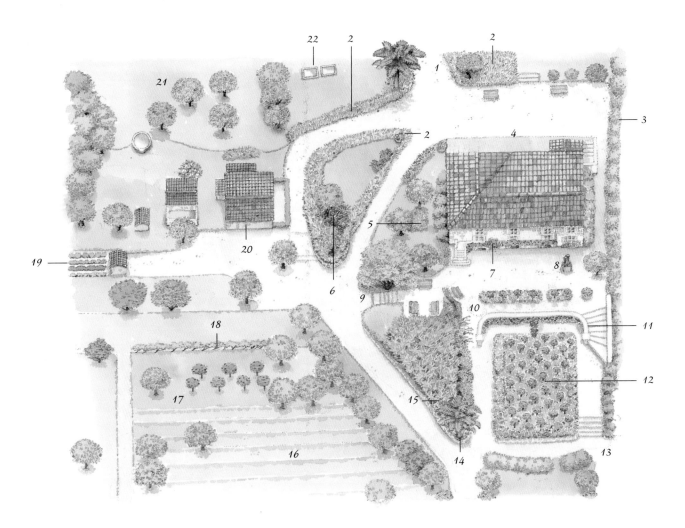

A SCHEME INSPIRED BY RENOIR'S
TERRACE PLANTING (RIGHT)
*Renoir loved to see orange-bearing trees
against a blue sky and he
underplanted citrus trees with blue
agapanthus along the terrace. Below
the terrace his wife planted roses and
lavender beneath citrus trees. Here
Valencia orange trees, underplanted
with alyssum, are surrounded by
'Hidcote' lavender interplanted with
roses and edged by lily grass (Liriope
spicata). The lavender could be
interplanted with tulips to give color in
the spring. Where citrus trees cannot be
left outside in the winter, hardy citrus
(Poncirus trifoliata), which has fragrant
yellow fruit, could be used instead.*

RIGHT A mature Judas tree shades the white gravel terrace and the assortment of terracotta pots and stone troughs outside Les Lauves, the house that Cézanne built on a hill leading out of Aix-en-Provence. His spacious studio is on the second floor.

OPPOSITE ABOVE No flowers are shown in Cézanne's watercolor Flower Pots (1883-7); the emphasis is on the pattern made by the twisting stems and ruffled leaves of the pelargoniums aligned on a shelf in his garden.

OPPOSITE BELOW A fruiting fig tree has been allowed to climb the walls of Les Lauves, partially concealing the doorway. A mature rosemary grows on the other side of the steps, above a collection of potted plants that include pelargonuims and spider plants . The garden that surrounds the house reflects Cézanne's interest in trees and woodland scenes.

ABOVE Cézanne painting in the country-side near his studio in Aix-en-Provence in 1906 shortly before his death.

large studio with an apartment above it where he could live, and cultivated a woodland garden on the slopes around the house. The site was within walking distance of the subject of so many of his landscapes – Mont Sainte-Victoire. Today markers direct visitors to a scenic country road where vistas of the mountain he cherished and painted come into view at every turn.

Cézanne's house and garden remain little changed from the day he died. A high stone wall conceals the property from the road; the heavy puce-colored door creaks slowly open to reveal a gravel driveway leading to a shaded patio area where marble blocks, like tomb stones, are used to display potted plants, and a flight of stone steps leads to the front door which is almost obscured by climbing plants.

Inside Cézanne's studio, skulls, conch shells, onions, apples and peaches are arranged among the pewterware he used in many of his still lifes. One large picture window has a spectacular view over the tops of the trees in his lower garden, while a second offers a glimpse, through a tangle of branches, of the upper garden behind the house.

In the garden the atmosphere is something like that in Renoir's olive

ABOVE *Self-portrait (1889) is one of the many self-portraits Van Gogh painted after he had moved from Paris to the south of France in 1888. He was thrilled with the landscape he found. "Nature here", he wrote to his brother, "[is] so extraordinarily beautiful." The blossoming of almond, plum and peach orchards, followed by the ripening wheatfields and vineyards inspired his painting and his palette.*

OPPOSITE *An old rose in a corner of the asylum garden at Saint-Rémy may be the same one described by Van Gogh as "a bush of pale roses in the cold shadow". Fragrant white mock orange (Philadelphus) flowers gleam in the background, while lustrous green leaves of bergenia spill over a raised border.*

orchard – tamed, but natural. It would be unfair to call Cézanne's garden neglected, for it is maintained by a full-time gardener, as it was in Cézanne's day, but it seems to overflow with trees and shrubs. The path which winds through them is like a labyrinth, repeatedly dividing and turning back on itself. It is almost entirely arched over by the branches of ivy-girdled trees and flowering or berry-bearing shrubs, reflecting Cézanne's love of leaf tunnels. Rough stone steps ascend a slope and descend to a flimsy rustic bridge made from tree branches which spans a stream. There are several stone seats – little more than massive flat slabs supported by rough square stones like those painted by Van Gogh in the asylum garden in nearby Saint-Rémy.

Like Cézanne and Renoir, Van Gogh was irresistibly drawn to the south of France, where he responded to the climate, landscape and vegetation with some of his most joyous and memorable work. Throughout what was to be a tragically short painting career of ten years, he found inspiration in gardens and plants. His father's somber parsonage garden, in his native Holland, attracted him first and he painted it even under gloomy, wintry skies. Later, when he moved south in 1888, he fell for the vibrant farm gardens on the outskirts of Arles, Provence, and he brightened his palette in a glorious celebration of the colors he saw. During the following year he was confined to an asylum at Saint-Rémy and in the garden there he completed some hundred works, many of which reflect his moods. Close-ups of poisonous hooded arums, death's head moths, menacing bottle-green beetles, and sinuous pine trees tethered with dark, suffocating ivy (see page 103) contrast with shimmering lilac trees and bright fields spangled with red poppies. Enclosed by a high stone wall, the garden of the asylum is little changed today; the pine trees are loftier and the lawns are now mown, but the massive stone seats are in exactly the same positions, and trails lead off into groves of towering oak trees.

Though the asylum garden is not open to the public, since it is still a psychiatric institution, there is a footpath around the grounds known as Van Gogh's Walk, leading to places that the artist painted. In nearby Arles, where he mutilated his ear following an argument with Gauguin, is the hospital where Van Gogh went for treatment. The colorful courtyard garden remains remarkably the same as when he depicted it from a balcony during his convalescence.

Of the many gardens at Auvers, near Paris, that Van Gogh painted during the last few months of his life in 1890, that of his doctor, Gachet, and that which had belonged to the artist Daubigny still survive, but these gardens are in private hands.

The gardens of Caillebotte, one of the most enthusiastic, hands-on gardeners among the Impressionists, have not fared so well. Caillebotte

A RECONSTRUCTION OF THE ARLES HOSPITAL GARDEN (OPPOSITE)
Using both Van Gogh's own description of the garden and his painting makes it possible to reconstruct the planting.

1   *Blue bearded irises*
2   *Forget-me-nots*
3   *Wallflowers*
4   *Oleander*
5   *Robinia pseudoacacia*
6   *Yucca*
7   *Pansies and ranunculus*
8   *Pansies, primroses, forget-me-nots, poppies*
9   *Pansies, primroses, forget-me-nots*
10   Anemone coronaria
11   *Hellebores and bergenia*
12   *Sweet violets*
13   Boxwood standards
14   *Shirley poppies and calendulas*
15   *Alyssum, meadowsweet (poached egg plant) and Iceland poppies*
16   *Goldfish pool with flag iris*

ABOVE AND RIGHT The hospital at Arles, now a crafts center and museum, has preserved the original design of its courtyard, which was described by Van Gogh as "an antique garden". It is laid out in a traditional pattern of radiating segments surrounded by a "plante bande", which is today filled with irises. Comparing the present-day photograph with Van Gogh's painting, The Garden of the Hospital at Arles *(1889), it is interesting to note that the artist felt it necessary to increase the size of the fish pond to satisfy his sense of composition on the canvas.*

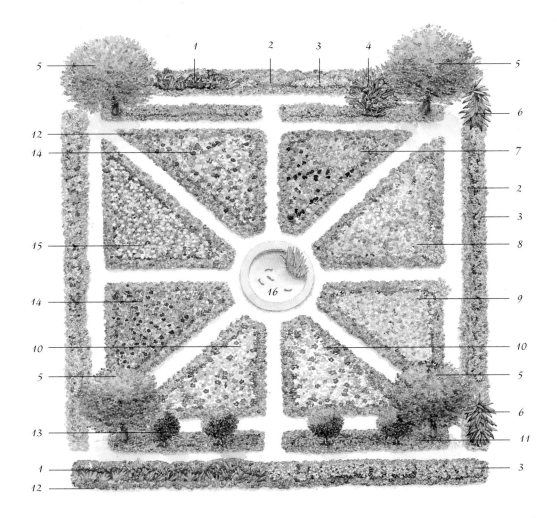

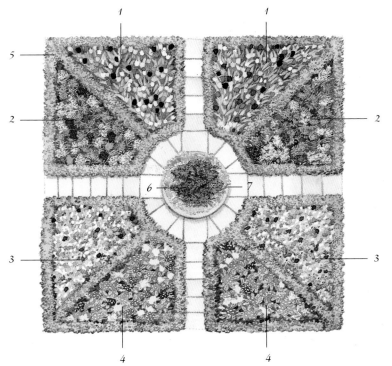

A PARTERRE BASED ON THE ARLES
HOSPITAL GARDEN (LEFT)

Much smaller in scale, and using less
tender plants than those that were in
the garden at Arles, this design has a
raised circular flower bed at its center
instead of a fountain. It does, however,
rely on seasonal bedding plants for its
sunburst of color. Here, it is seen in the
spring.

1 Tulipa 'Triumphator'
2 Hyacinths
3 Majestic Giant pansies
4 Pacific series polyanthus
5 Sweet violets
6 Myosotis 'Carmine King'
7 Myosotis 'Blue Bird'

OPPOSITE *In* The Kitchen Garden at Yerres *(c. 1877) Caillebotte uses muted colors to capture the hazy atmosphere of a quiet, misty morning in his family's formal fruit and vegetable garden. A circular well at the intersection of the main paths makes a good focal point; it was also of practical use as a source of water in the center of the plot. The orderliness of the rows of plants and the use of the wall space on which to train fruit trees are typical of productive gardens at the end of the nineteenth century. Caillebotte was to lay out his own garden at Petit-Gennevillers in a similar geometric pattern, to satisfy his passion for strong lines of perspective.*

ABOVE *Though part of the kitchen garden at Yerres has been lost to a parking lot, long rows of beans, lettuces, tomatoes and other vegetables are still grown in regimented lines just as they were portrayed by Caillebotte.*

must have learned a good deal of his horticultural expertise from the gardeners who worked on his family's twenty-seven-acre estate at Yerres, south-east of Paris. The extensive gardens were the subject of many of his paintings (see page 10). The colonnaded Italianate house, and a Swiss chalet-style guest cottage with gingerbread trim, together with portions of the one-acre walled kitchen garden, still survive as a public park, but are sadly in need of repair and restoration.

Following the death of his mother in 1879, the estate at Yerres was sold and Caillebotte, then aged thirty-one, moved to a property on the banks of the River Seine, at Petit-Gennevilliers, north-west of Paris. There he cultivated flowers, fruit and vegetables in a substantial, highly formal garden of about an acre. Like Monet, he was passionate about plants (indeed he is credited with developing Monet's interest in gardening). He was a keen collector of roses and dahlias, and also raised orchids in a conservatory. Caillebotte's paintings are noted for their exaggerated lines of perspective, and this perhaps explains the intricate methods he used for training his fruit trees. The skilfully pruned trees also allowed him to compress a lot of plants into a relatively confined space and to harvest the produce more easily. Personally, I find Caillebotte's espalier, fan, cordon and Belgian fence patterns so space-saving and beautiful, that after first seeing them, I tore up my own recently planted fruit trees and devised a new orchard, using mostly dwarf varieties, to emulate Caillebotte's magnificent designs.

Both Pissarro and Sisley were drawn to kitchen gardens as subjects for their paintings and Pissarro cultivated both produce and flowers in his walled garden at Eragny, north-west of Paris. Unfortunately neither this garden, nor Sisley's own cramped city garden survive.

As the influence of Impressionism spread, Giverny attracted a large number of painters, particularly from America, headed by John Singer Sargent. The American Impressionist, Theodore Robinson, purchased a house next door to Monet, and they became close friends. A friend of Robinson's, another American Impressionist painter, Theodore Butler, married two of Monet's step-daughters – first Suzanne, who died of illness, and then Martha.

Frederick C. Frieseke, another American-born Impressionist, later moved into Robinson's house and Frieseke's wife cultivated a magnificent garden. Though inspired more by Renoir's sensuous paintings of women, Frieseke's romantic garden scenes, such as *Lilies* (see page 130), helped establish him as the leader of the second generation of American Impressionists. Frieseke's house and garden still survive as a private residence, owned by Daniel J. Terra who founded, on an adjacent property, the Musée Americain, Giverny.

Among the work of the foreigners who visited France and studied art,

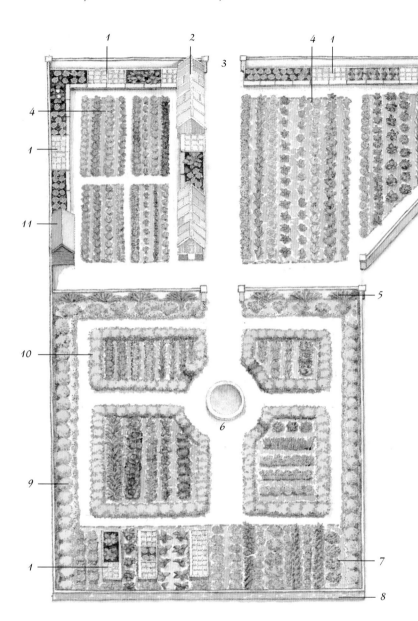

THE CAILLEBOTTE KITCHEN GARDEN AT YERRES

1   Cold frame
2   Greenhouses
3   Entrance from estate
4   Vegetable crops
5   Espaliered fruit trees
6   Well
7   Small fruits and vegetables
8   Wall enclosure
9   Strawberries edging fruit trees
10 Currant and gooseberry bushes
11 Garden shed

ABOVE RIGHT Caillebotte (kneeling) and a gardener at work in his garden at Petit-Gennevilliers. Traditionally laid out in geometric shapes, the beds featured fruit trees trained on wooden supports to gain maximum production from minimum space.

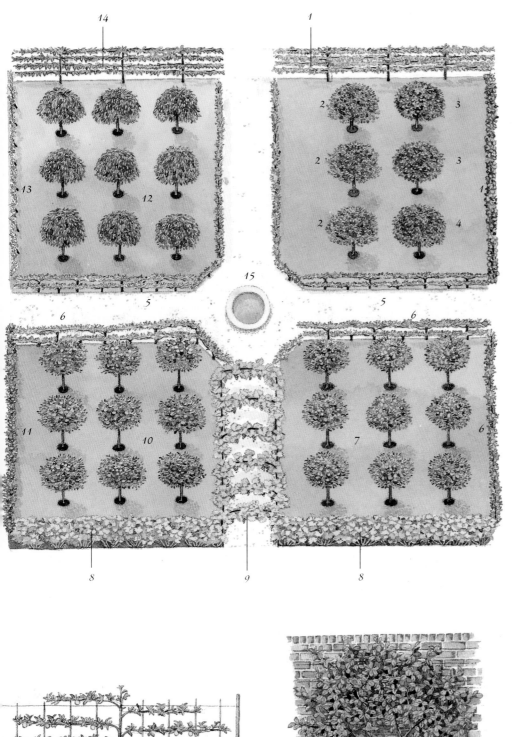

This orchard , which is only 18m (60ft) square, is based on Caillebotte's trained fruit trees. All the apples are grafted onto EM IX, EM II or EM 26 dwarf rooting stock; all the pears are grafted onto EM A dwarf rooting stock (hardy quince). The Belgian fence and espaliered apples and pears have a strong scaffold of bamboo poles, the peaches and nectarines are fanned out along a framework of strong wire, and the cordon apples and pears are trained along low wooden rails.

1   Espaliered peach trees
2   Plum trees
3   Apricot trees
4   'Star Stella' cherry tree
5   Horizontal cordon apple trees
6   Horizontal cordon pear trees
7   Spindle-pruned pear trees
8   Horizontal-trained grape vines
9   Grape arbor
10 Spindle pruned apple trees
11 Espaliered apples
12 Peach trees
13 Belgian fence apple trees
14 Espaliered nectarine trees
15 Well head.

TRAINED FRUIT TREES (BELOW)
These types of fruit training are based on those used in the Caillebotte gardens at Yerres and Petit-Gennevilliers: (from left to right) Belgian fence – for apples, pears and peaches; espalier – for apples, pears, grapes, brambles; fan – for peaches, nectarines, plums, figs and brambles; double tier of single tier espalier – for apples and pears.

RIGHT *Hassam's pastel,* Hollyhocks, Isles of Shoals *(1902), is one of many drawings and paintings he did of Celia Thaxter's cutting garden which overlooks the Atlantic Ocean on an exposed cliff top in Maine. The other flowers appear to be blue larkspur* (Consolida ambigua)*, red and white Shirley poppies* (Papaver rhoeas) *and yellow crown daisies* (Chrysanthemum coronarium).

BELOW *Hassam painting on the porch of Celia Thaxter's house on Appledore Island, Maine, where, from 1890, he spent part of every summer for twenty-two years.*

the paintings of American-born Childe Hassam perhaps come closest to French Impressionism. Some of his garden- and seascapes are comparable to those of Monet, in spite of the fact that he never visited Giverny and always denied being influenced by Monet's work. Although there are many garden scenes in Hassam's oeuvre, he has come to be most closely associated with a flower garden on Appledore Island, off the coast of Maine. There he enjoyed the hospitality of poet and gardener Celia Thaxter who had attended his watercolor classes in Boston. "I plant my garden to pick, not for show," she declared, but she might have added "and also to be painted", for some of Hassam's most evocative and celebrated images are of her garden, and illustrate her book, *An Island Garden* (1894, facsimile reprint 1988).

In the book Thaxter gives a detailed account of the flowers she grew, and explains why particular flowers won space in her garden, peppering the text with interesting gardening tips. Her love of poppies reflects their importance in Hassam's work, and occupies an entire chapter, covering the benefits of Shirley poppies ("they are the tenderest lilac, the deepest crimson, richest scarlet, white and softest suffusion of rose ..."), Iceland poppies ("from the frosty fields of Greenland, in buttercup yellow and orange and white"), the large Oriental poppy ("there is a kind of angry brilliance about it"), and the golden California poppies ("yellow of many resplendent shades").

Hassam's paintings of Thaxter's cutting garden make it seem large, but actually it occupied a rectangular space only 4.5 metres (15 feet) wide by 15 metres (50 feet) long; yet it yielded a hundred or more bouquets of freshly cut flowers each week.

Though the clapboard house that immediately overlooked the garden has long since perished by fire, the garden itself has been faithfully restored following the original planting plans, and is now open to the public. When one stands in her garden, looking towards the ocean, engulfed by the colors and scents of a thousand flowers, it is not hard to understand why Thaxter would go into her garden at 5 o'clock each morning, before anyone else was awake, to find, as she described it, "... a silent joy that fills me with infinite content".

BELOW Though Hassam captured many exhilarating seascapes on Appledore Island showing dramatic sunsets, rocky headlands and choppy seas, his favorite motif was clumps of poppies growing along the cliff walks. The blue sea and sky still make a pleasing background color for the pastel-pink poppies.

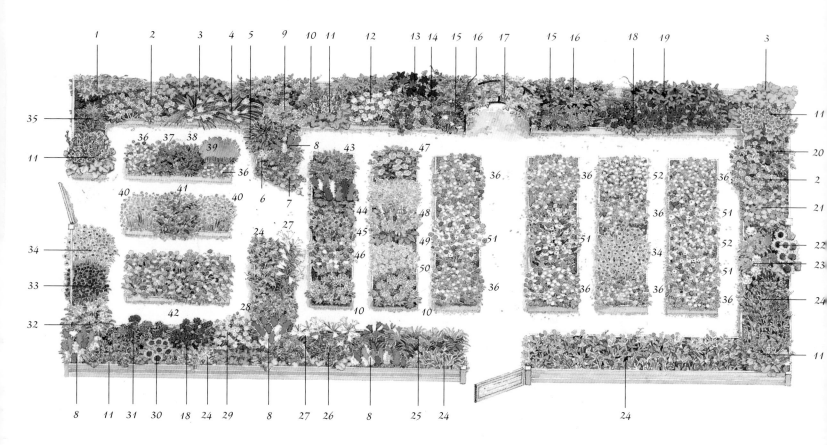

CELIA THAXTER'S CUTTING GARDEN

1 Akebia quinata
2 Rosa × damascena
3 Humulus japonicus
4 Hemerocallis citrina
5 Weigela florida
6 Iberis sempervirens
7 Tropaeolum majus
8 Consolida ambigua
9 Cleome hassleriana
10 Lonicera japonica
11 Alcea rosea
12 Echinocystis lobata
13 Clematis × jackmanii
14 Rosa *hybrids*
15 Verbena × hybrida
16 Lonicera sempervirens
17 Wisteria sinensis
18 *Red dahlias*
19 Clematis 'Henryi'
20 Papaver orientale

21 Tagetes erecta
22 Helianthus annuus
23 Phlox paniculata
24 Lathyrus odoratus
25 Lilium *Asiatic hybrids*
26 Lavatera trimestris
27 Lilium longiflorum
28 Aquilegia vulgaris
29 Rosa pimpinellifolia
30 Helianthus × multiflorus
31 Dianthus barbatus
32 Paeonia lactiflora *(silvery-pink)*
33 Centaurea cyanus
34 Coreopsis tinctoria
35 *Sweet violets*
36 Callistephus chinensis
37 Eschscholzia californica
38 *Wallflowers*
39 Lavendula angustifolia
40 Linum perenne
41 Silene coeli-rosa

42 Papaver nudicaule
43 Clematis terniflora
44 Delphinium *hybrids*
45 Nigella damascena
46 Papaver somniferum
47 Paeonia lactiflora *(pink)*
48 Dianthus plumarius
49 Digitalis purpurea
50 Coreopsis grandiflora
51 *Shirley poppies*
52 Reseda odorata

OPPOSITE *The raised beds defined by wooden boards in Celia Thaxter's restored cutting garden bring a sense of order into the mass of densely planted flowers – here pink asters, yellow coreopsis and blue cornflowers. The metal arch once led to her front porch (see page 114).*

COLOR AND LIGHT

PREVIOUS PAGES In The Artist's Garden at Giverny *(1900), Monet shows clumps of bi-colored bearded irises beneath young crab apple and cherry trees on a sunny day, and has translated patterns of light and shade made by the trees into pure color. At Giverny today, in early June, purple and pale blue and white bearded irises combine with pink and white dame's rocket* (Hesperis matronalis) *and mauve aubrietia to create a harmonious, shimmering pastel color scheme, while deep pink peonies and red standard roses prevent it from looking insipid.*

BELOW The Impressionists discovered some of their most striking ideas for color schemes in natural effects. On a clear day, a stream at Cedaridge Farm reveals a conjunction of yellow and blue – from reflections of autumn leaves and blue sky – a color contrast much admired by the Impressionists.

Over a century after the first Impressionist exhibition was such a *cause célèbre* in Paris and when how and what the artists painted has long since ceased to be controversial, Impressionist exhibitions still draw record crowds, and the paintings command record prices at art auctions. Perhaps part of their enduring appeal lies in their extraordinary use of colors – particularly the brightness and freshness we still see in them.

The Impressionists were the first painters to translate light into color and to model in subtle gradations of color rather then in contrasts of light and shade. Their intense observations of nature and the changes made by the play of light on color from moment to moment and through all seasons led the Impressionists to express the idea that objects do not have a true color because all colors are affected by the dynamics of light and by the color of other objects in close proximity. When the paintings were first exhibited in Paris, these concepts were grounds for ridicule from critics who judged artistic merit by its degree of "realism" and by popular notions of color.

The scientific theories behind most of the Impressionists' color observations had been formulated and published as early as 1839, and they remain the principles that still govern our response to color. For gardeners today – as it was for the Impressionists – it is by combining an understanding of these academic theories with direct observations from nature that the most successful color schemes can be created. The iris, for example – a flower that captivated both Van Gogh and Monet – is so diverse in its range of colors, and the colors themselves vary so much according to changes in light that they almost defy classification; and it is perhaps these permutations of color in nature that prompted both Monet and Renoir to declare a horror of the scientific theory, while accepting that an education in color theory was necessary for sound artistic training.

Van Gogh perhaps expressed the value of theories best when he wrote to his younger sister, Wilhelmina, from Provence: "Explaining the whole theory to you would involve quite a lot of writing, yet it might be done. Colorings, wallpapers, and whatnot would be made much prettier by paying attention to the laws of colors." These laws of colors had been developed and codified by Michel-Eugène Chevreul, director of dye quality control at the Gobelins tapestry workshops, in his book *The Principles of Harmony and Contrast of Colors*. He included a color wheel showing the scientific relationship between colors and how the three primary colors – red, yellow and blue – can be used to make all the secondary colors by being mixed in varying proportions (red and yellow will make orange, for example, and blue and red will make violet). Chevreul's principal thesis was that colors in proximity influence and modify one another (red, for example, will look quite different when it is juxtaposed with green than with blue); complementary colors are those directly opposite each other on the wheel and make the strongest contrasts when they are placed together; and that any color on its own appears to be surrounded by a faint aureole of its complementary color. He noted how colors mix optically with each other so that when two threads of different colors are entwined, for instance, they appear to be a single color.

These theories were explored by the Impressionists who tinged shadows with colors complementary to those of the object casting the shadows; and they built up their canvases in small touches of pure color to express the constant changes in the play of light. Both Monet and Caillebotte owned copies of Chevreul's book, and color theory was debated intensely among the Impressionists, but how much they were influenced is not clear, since Monet himself insisted his inspiration was drawn more from nature than scientific analysis. "I agree...that all the arts have points in common, that there are harmonies and concerts that are self-sufficient and that affect us as a musical phrase or chord can strike us deeply, without reference to a precise or clearly stated theory", he wrote to art critic, Roger Marx. Monet did, however, possess another highly influential book on color theory in the garden which is believed to have given both Monet and Caillebotte (and certainly Gertrude Jekyll) food for thought. *Manuel de l'Amateur de Jardin* was published in 1864 by two French garden writers, Decaisne and Naudin, who elaborated Chevreul's scientific color theories further and carried them into the garden. Their book explained their philosophy of color combinations: "All primary colors, when pure, contrast pleasantly with each other. In the same way complementary colors contrast with each other to great advantage," they declared. They gave as examples of beauty the coupling of yellow and purple, of red and green and of blue and orange.

Van Gogh came to similar conclusions about color in the garden. Although he never created a garden of his own, Van Gogh was an acute observer of color in nature and its effects in the garden, and expressed his ideas in letters to his brother and sister: "Spring", he enthused to his brother Theo, "is tender young shoots of wheat and pink apple blossoms. Autumn is the contrast of yellow leaves with shades of violet. Winter is white with black silhouettes. If summer is taken to be a contrast of blues with the orange of golden, bronze grain, it is possible to paint a picture in complementary colors for every one of the seasons."

In a subsequent letter to his sister, Van Gogh suggested how these theories could be put into practice in her garden in Holland: "Cornflowers and white chrysanthemums and a certain number of marigolds...a motif in blue and orange....Heliotrope and yellow roses – motif

This simple color wheel shows the three primary colors – red, yellow and blue – and the three secondary colors – violet (a mix of blue and red), green (a mix of yellow and blue) and orange (a mix of red and yellow) – with the intermediary colors that link them. Colors directly opposite each other on the color wheel, known as complementary colors, make the strongest contrasts when they are placed next to each other, while colors that are close to each other on the wheel are harmonious. The prevailing interest in scientific color theory was the milieu in which the Impressionists evolved their use of color; however, in practise they relied far more on their own intense observations of nature. As Cézanne observed, "Monet is only an eye – but what an eye."

in lilac and yellow .... Poppies and red geraniums in vigorous green leaves – motif in red and green .... These are fundamentals that one may subdivide further, and elaborate, but quite enough to show you without the help of a picture that there are colors which cause each other to shine brilliantly, which form a *couple*, which complete each other like man and woman."

Twelve years earlier Monet had begun to experiment with his own color theories in gardens he cultivated on rented properties; first at Argenteuil, close to Paris, and then at Vétheuil, further north, before his final move to Giverny in 1883. *Gladioli* (1876) painted at Argenteuil, is dominated by the tall spires of red flowers and green leaves, while *Flowerbeds at Vétheuil* (1881), shows a more dramatic planting of tall yellow sunflowers and creeping orange nasturtiums shining against a blue sweep of the River Seine. The predominantly red and green scheme in the first painting, and the yellow, orange and blue scheme in the other two paintings are the same complementary color combinations that Van Gogh recommended to his sister.

Monet was to develop these color schemes in his much more elaborate garden at Giverny. A British journalist who visited Monet

BELOW Van Gogh's Irises *(1889), painted within a week of his arrival at the asylum at Saint-Rémy, exemplifies his concern with complementary colors. The blue irises contrast vividly with the bright orange calendulas and the darker rust tones of the earth.*

OPPOSITE The blues and greens in this border of perennials and annuals echoes those used by Van Gogh. The yellow tagetes, coreopsis, helenium, achilleas and frothy Alchemilla mollis *make gentle contrasts with the mauves of salvia and erigeron and with the strong blue of the delphiniums.*

described the yellow and blue color contrast that he saw there as "the gold and sapphire of an artist's dreams." It was present in spring in plantings of blue bearded iris massed among yellow and orange English wallflowers; and yellow daisy-like leopard's bane *(Doronicum orientale)* planted with the honesty *(Lunaria annua).* In summer the scheme continued with annual blue and purple morning glories *(Ipomoea purpurea)* mingled with yellow and orange nasturtiums *(Tropaeolum majus),* and in autumn with golden perennial sunflowers *(Helianthus salicifolius)* above clumps of blue perennial New England asters *(Aster novae-angliae).*

The "gold and sapphire" colors that Monet used were essentially the complementary colors yellow and purple; used together in the garden they make stunning combinations. Indeed, most of the range of blues and purples look good with yellow, as the Impressionists discovered. Like Monet did in his garden, it is possible to maintain this color scheme all through the year, beginning perhaps with yellow 'Hawera' daffodils above blue Siberian squill *(Scilla siberica),* a combination which would look especially beautiful beneath yellow forsythia. In a shady area Spanish bluebells *(Hyacinthoides hispanica)* would do well around a yellow Mollis azalea. These might be followed by blue forget-me-nots *(Myosotis* 'Blue Bird') and blue columbines *(Aquilegia alpina)* with yellow tulips such as *Tulipa* 'West Point', a lily-flowered tulip. Then, when the bulbs are over, they could be replaced with a planting of annuals. A classic combination would be blue lobelia *(L. erinus* 'Crystal Palace') with yellow petunias *(P.* 'California Girl') and creamy-yellow snapdragons *(Antirrhinum majus* Madam Butterfly series). Alternatively, blue Swan River daisies *(Brachyscome iberidifolia),* which have yellow centers, could be teamed with corn marigolds *(Chrysanthemum segetum).* Among blue or violet perennials, perhaps the most valuable for their color are varieties of salvia and veronica. *Salvia* × *sylvestris* 'May Night' is a deep violet-blue and *Veronica spicata incana* a deep blue; they would make superb companions for yellow loosestrife *(Lysimachia punctata),* 'Early Sunrise' coreopsis and pale yellow foxgloves *(Digitalis lutea).* Other useful blue and yellow plants which display their flowers on tall spires include hybrid delphiniums, which come in all shades of blue, as well as a yellow ('Sungleam'); blue larkspur *(Consolida ambigua);* violet-blue balloon flowers *(Platycodon grandiflorus);* yellow mullein *(Verbascum olympicum),* yolk-yellow foxtail lilies *(Eremurus stenophyllus)* and creamy *Sisyrinchium striatum.*

A mix of blue and yellow can be carried a storey higher by entwining blue clematis with a yellow climbing rose. Lavender-blue *Clematis* 'Ramona', for example, could grow through *Rosa* 'Graham Thomas', or deeper blue *Clematis* 'H.F. Young' wind through the small pale lemon flowers of *Rosa banksiae* 'Lutea'.

Monet's Field of Yellow Irises *(1887) shows a flat, swampy area near his house in Giverny where wild yellow flag iris* (Iris pseudacorus) *established large colonies. Using blues and violets to suggest shadows among the iris foliage and in the tree line on the horizon, Monet creates a stunning color scheme. There also appear to be smaller colonies of blue flag iris* (Iris versicolor) *in the background. These two wild irises still bloom today in the low-lying meadows around Giverny.*

Bright spires of yellow loosestrife (Lysimachia punctata) *tower above violet-blue spikes of* Veronica spicata *'Goodness Grows' and deep violet* Salvia nemorosa *'Lubecca' in a yellow and violet-blue scheme in one of the sunny perennial borders at Cedaridge Farm. Pale lavender shades of* Phlox *'Chattahoochee' and an early flowering* Boltonia *'Pink Beauty' spill over an edging of silvery-blue* Artemisia stelleriana *'Silver Brocade'.*

For later in the year blue spiraea *(Caryopteris incana)* might be surrounded with autumn daffodils *(Sternbergia lutea)* and yellow dahlias such as 'Lady Linda'. Asters are among the longest-flowering perennials and, taking a lead from Giverny, try planting *Aster novi-belgii* 'Purple Dome' with perennial sunflowers *(Helianthus salicifolius)*.

Although blue is the true complement of orange, a true blue is rare in nature since most flowers must contrast with the color of the sky in order to attract pollinators. Instead, orange can be teamed with violet, indigo and lavender-blues to make arresting combinations – think of deep purple *Delphinium* 'Black Knight' with an orange lily such as 'Enchantment' or *Clematis × jackmanii* climbing above *Rosa* 'Orangeade'. Using apricot shades instead of orange obviously makes softer contrasts with the blues.

An exciting scheme of complementary and near-complementary colors can be produced using just one flower family, such as pansies which were particularly popular with the Impressionists. Pansies have yellow, orange, cream and apricot in their color range as well as light blue, sky blue, violet, purple, lavender and maroon.

Petunias are another good family of flowers rich in blue and yellow shades. As the yellow is a recent addition by flower breeders, perhaps a more authentic period planting would be to combine an assortment of violet-blue petunias with yellow, orange and apricot nasturtiums. The Multiflora class of single-flowered petunias and the spurless Whirlybird range of bushy nasturtiums make particularly good companions.

A BLUE/VIOLET AND ORANGE/YELLOW PATHSIDE PLANTING (BELOW) Inspired by Van Gogh's Irises *(see page 44), this scheme features yellow, blue and violet bearded irises in combination with orange pot marigolds and California poppies . White and blue forget-me-nots edge the path and a few more are scattered among the groups of iris. Iris rhizomes like to be exposed to the sun and so dwarf 'Blue Heaven' delphiniums and 'Mönch' perennial blue asters, which will flower later in the summer, are planted behind the irises. Lobelia could replace the forget-me-nots, and later yellow and orange might come from French marigolds, nasturtiums and yellow and gold dahlias.*

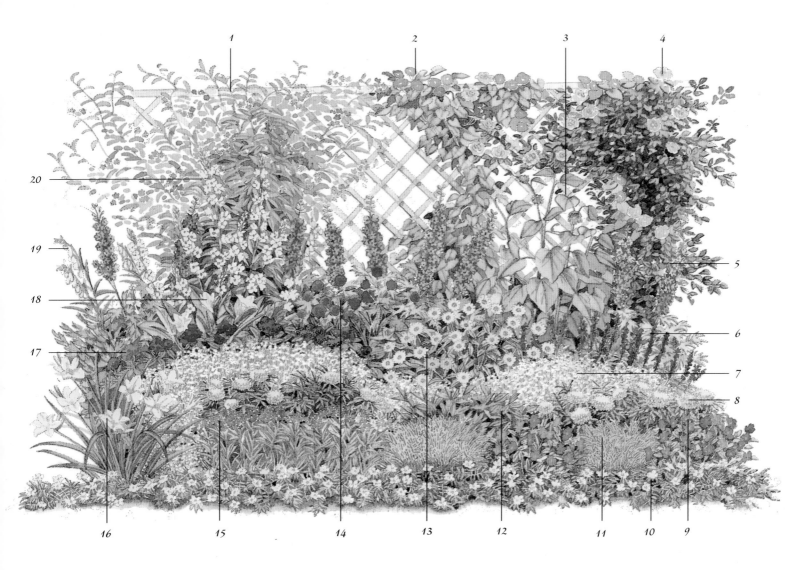

A BLUE AND YELLOW BORDER
Based on a combination of colors admired especially by Monet and Van Gogh, this border of 2.5 × 5.5 m (8 × 18 ft) is shown in mid-summer. Earlier color would have come from primroses, daffodils, irises, columbines and forget-me-nots. A few blue late flowering shrubs and perennials, such as Russian sage (Perovskia), Caryopteris × clandonensis and asters, would be a good addition to the border, while the yellow hues might come from Cosmos sulphureus, rudbeckia, dahlias and zinnias.

1 Solanum crispum *'Glasnevin'*
2 Ipomoea purpurea *'Heavenly Blue'*
3 Helianthus annuus
4 Rosa *'Golden Showers'*
5 Delphinium *'Summer Skies'*
6 Salvia farinacea *'Victoria'*
7 Gypsophila paniculata
8 Tagetes erecta *'Inca Yellow'*
9 Viola *'Blue Gem'*
10 Tagetes signata *'Lemon Gem'*
11 Cosmos sulphureus *foliage*
12 Rudbeckia *foliage*
13 Coreopsis *'Early Sunrise'*
14 Echinops ritro

15 Cynoglossum amabile
16 Hemerocallis *'Marion Vaughn'*
17 Heliotropium *'Marine'*
18 Lilium *'Connecticut King'*
19 Digitalis lutea
20 Verbascum chaixii

Renoir's paintings are also rich in orange-and-blue and yellow-and-blue combinations, particularly his images of the south of France, such as *Landscape near Menton* (1883) which shows two ancient yellow-tinted olive trees and yellow meadow grasses on a clifftop overlooking the blue Mediterranean. One of his favorite colors, however, was red, and in many of his garden scenes red and green predominate. *Garden at Fontanay* (1874) shows two women among red roses, and *Flowers and Cats* (1881) depicts pots of startling red pelargoniums massed in a large china container.

The dramatic possibilities inherent in a red and green garden were seen by Manet, most famously in *The Bench* (1881). In the paintings of another, unassuming, garden of a house he rented towards the end of his life, he added touches of bright red – probably from bedding geraniums – to enliven what would otherwise have been a largely green scene. Nowhere, perhaps, is the vibrant contrast made by red and green better seen than in the iridescent wild poppies immortalized in the fields of Normandy by Monet, in the orchards of Provence by Van Gogh, and on the cliff tops of Maine by Hassam.

Van Gogh thought that red and green seemed to express all the world's anger. Celia Thaxter wrote that red Oriental poppies had an angry aura. Red and green is not an easy combination to handle, but an enticing red and green garden can be seen today in Giverny at the

OPPOSITE *Manet's best-known garden painting,* The Bench *(1881), was completed during a week of continuous rain when he was discouraged from wandering further afield than the garden of a house he rented in Versailles. The green-painted bench and treillage and plentiful green foliage provide an effective background for the red flowers – bedding geraniums and dahlias, and an end-of-summer rose. The warm colors of the path and mulched earth are echoed in the russet tinges given to the dahlias.*

ABOVE *'Paul's Scarlet Climber' rose combines with red pansies to create a strong complementary scheme of green and red at Giverny. By placing hot colors – like this red – in the foreground, and pale, cooler colors further back, Monet created an illusion of greater distance.*

A predominantly red and green planting at Cedaridge Farm uses tulips in front of a trellised arch in spring. The bi-colored white and red tulips (T. 'Garden Party') at the center create a shimmering sensation, especially when backlit. After the tulips are over, the red roses that climb over the arch come into bloom at the same time as Salvia coccinea 'Lady in Red', red 'Nonstop' tuberous begonias and red 'Elfin' impatiens, which are planted in the lightly shaded beds.

home of painter Jean-Marie Toulgouat, a descendant of Theodore Butler and Monet's step-daughter, Suzanne. Monsieur Toulgouat uses a rich array of leaf shapes and sizes as a foil for heavily scented crimson roses that seem positively to glow among the greenery. The plants in his garden that are grown chiefly for their foliage are feathery lady ferns, shiny green bergenias, fountain-like clumps of daylilies, lace-like snakeroot *(Cimicifuga* species*)* and hogweed *(Heracleum mantegazzianum)* with its massive, deeply indented leaves. Other plants that are useful for their foliage include undulating hostas, hellebores and fluffy fennel.

Both Monet and Van Gogh were attracted by the conjunction of red with silvery grey as well as green that they chanced upon in the countryside. In *Poppy Field near Giverny* (1885) Monet portrayed the grey tones of wild sage growing just beyond the walls of his garden; and in *Field with Poppies* (1889) Van Gogh captured the light reflecting from the rows of grey lavender foliage that grew beyond the walls of the asylum at Saint-Rémy. Perhaps recognizing that red and grey is not an easy combination to use in the garden, Monet added pink to the scheme when he planted the island beds immediately in front of his house at Giverny. He edged the beds with silver-leaved dianthus and filled them with red pelargoniums and pink standard roses.

A RED AND GREEN COURTYARD GARDEN

Inspired by Manet's painting The Bench *and based on the structure of a New Zealand garden designed by Olive Dunn, this small enclosed garden of about 6 × 9 m (20 × 30 ft) needs a lot of good foliage as a backdrop for the brightly colored flowers. It is shown here in summer; earlier color would have come from tulips and deep claret Cowichan primulas; while evergreen plants help to give year-round interest.*

1 Rosa *'Papa Mailland'*
2 Rosa *'Paul's Scarlet Climber'*
3 Lathyrus odoratus
4 Pyracantha coccinea
5 Rosa *'Westerland'*
6 Ivy-leaved pelargonium
7 Rosa *'Crimson Glory'*
8 Campsis × tagliabuana *'Madame Galen'*
9 Ipomoea *'Scarlett O'Hara'*
10 Chaenomeles × superba
11 Clematis *'Ville de Lyon'*
12 Rosa *'Fragrant Cloud'*
13 Primula foliage
14 Viola *'Arkwright's Ruby'*
15 Heuchera *'Palace Purple'*
16 Zinnia *'Rose Pinwheel'*
17 Helleborus orientalis
18 Nicotiana alata
19 Viola *'Crimson Queen'*
20 Fuchsia *'Mary Poppins'*
21 Thymus vulgaris
22 Ajuga reptans *'Atropurpurea'*
23 Gladiolus
24 Lobularia maritima

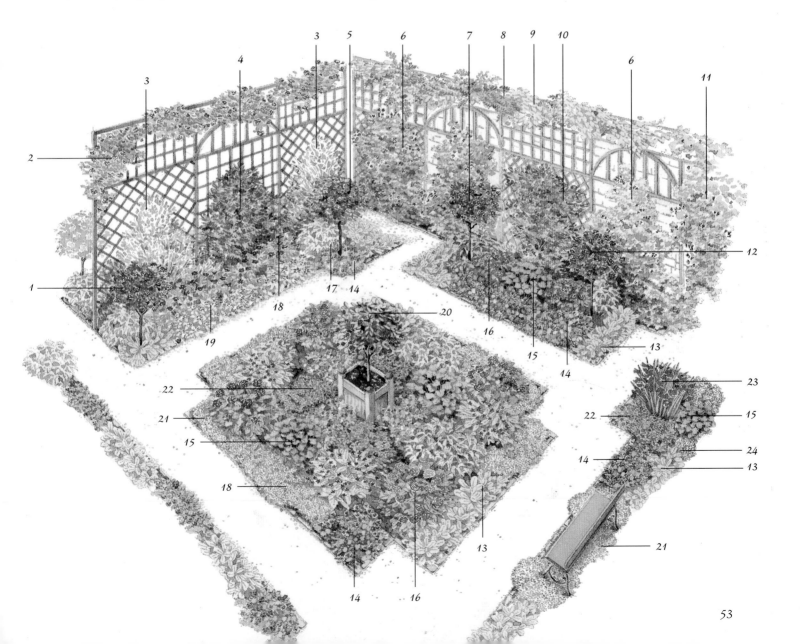

Other low-growing silvery-grey plants that could be used for edging include dwarf cotton lavender *(Santolina chamaecyparissus* var. *nana)* and *Senecio cineraria,* and low-growing artemisias like 'Silver Brocade'. For taller accents, *Artemesia* 'Powis Castle' has some of the best silvery coloration and provides a good foil for pink roses and lilies.

Chevreul's spectral wheel can be divided into ranges of warm colors (orange, yellow, red) and cool colors (blue, turquoise and violet, for example). These are groups of colors adjacent to each other on the wheel. Colors that are closely related are usually known as harmonious colors. Not only did Monet arrange the paints on his palette in warm and cool colors, but he also used these harmonies in his garden at Giverny. Monet was a master of painting sunrises and sunsets, recognizing that in the cool of the morning even reds and yellows can be muted, especially when veiled in mist. At the other extreme, the concentration of rays from a setting sun can infuse colors with warm reddish tones, making hot colors even hotter.

In the garden Monet used these phenomena to spectacular effect, planting the western side of his Grande Allée with orange, gold, yellow, bronze and red wallflowers. The backlighting from a setting sun would turn these colors into glowing orange, molten gold, burnished bronze, liquid yellow and fiery red.

Reflecting Chevreul's color wheel, Monet divided the paints on his palette into warm colors – such as red, orange and yellow – and cool colors – such as green, blue and violet. In many of his earlier garden paintings, Monet used warm colors tempered by expanses of cool blue sky or water. In these three paintings (ABOVE), he uses warm color harmonies to fill the whole of his canvas. (LEFT) Monet's Garden at Giverny (1895), (CENTER) The Rose Walk (1922) which shows a view along his Grande Allée and (RIGHT) The House from the Garden (1922) are scenes of his garden at Giverny.

Towards the end of his life, during a period of treatment for cataracts – when he painted the second two of these three paintings – Monet experienced color distortions and blurred vision, causing him to see only in shades of red, orange

and yellow. (At another stage of his treatment he saw only shades of blue.) In spite of his handicap from near blindness, and distress at the thought of losing his sight, Monet continued to paint – ironically producing some sensational, revolutionary work, more modernist than Impressionist.

One of Van Gogh's most admired paintings *The Red Vineyard* (1888) – the only painting he ever sold in his lifetime – shows how intense an effect the combination of a setting sun and a light shower of rain can have on the hot colors of an autumnal landscape. In a letter to his brother, Van Gogh explained "... on Sunday if you had been with us, you would have seen a red vineyard, all red like red wine. In the distance it turned to yellow, and then a green sky with the sun, the earth after the rain violet, sparkling yellow here and there where it caught the reflection of the setting sun ..."

The warm, hot colors such as orange and yellow are notoriously difficult to use effectively – particularly in small spaces – because they tend to assert themselves and dominate everything else in the garden. The warm colors are somehow easiest to look at in the spring when narcissi and tulips flower among the greens of freshly unfurled leaves, and again in autumn when deciduous trees lend their russet colors to the scene. However, since more orange and yellow flowers bloom in summer it is useful to find interesting ways to use them.

The addition of cream flowers can help to soften the powerful effect of hot colors, while the inclusion of very dark colors can also knock back the brilliance. Van Gogh was drawn to the contrast of orange and black in his paintings of a flower garden in Provence. The combination of

Warm, or hot, color harmonies can be created with bulbs and annuals, shrubs, and perennials.

LEFT ABOVE A simple companion planting of orange-red 'Allegro' Oriental poppies and bi-colored red and yellow 'Paris' tulips in Monet's garden. 'Allegro', developed by a French seedsman, is a dwarf, early-flowering type of Oriental poppy that comes into bloom at the same time as late single-flowered tulips.

LEFT BELOW The Exbury and Knap Hill strains of hybrid azaleas contain many beautiful shades of red, yellow and orange that can be combined to create a magnificent color harmony for a lightly shaded location. Here 'Barbara Jackman', 'Sham's Yellow', 'Supreme' and 'Gold Ducat' grow with white 'Nancy Buchanan'. They have the bonus of pleasant fragrance.

RIGHT Deeper tones and shades have been included in this border to temper the brilliance of its warm colors. A purple smoke bush (Cotinus coggygria), dark crimson dahlias (D. 'Blaisdon Red') and the almost black centers of orange heleniums and yellow rudbeckia mingle with yellow achillea, red hot pokers (Kniphofia uvaria 'Nobilis') and crocosmia. The colors used in this scheme compare with the "sunset" borders planted by Monet, while the planting in bold drifts is more typical of Gertrude Jekyll. Monet and Jekyll shared a liking for similar color themes, and although Jekyll certainly sought inspiration from Impressionist paintings – she is often referred to as "the first Impressionist horticulturist" – there are differences in their planting styles (see text on page 68).

A WARM COLOR BORDER (ABOVE)
Based on one of the "sunset" borders at Giverny, this bed would look its best if it could be placed so that it was backlit by the setting sun.

1   Malus × schiedeckeri *'Red Jade'*
2   *Mollis hybrid azaleas*
3   Doronicum orientale
4   *Wallflowers*
5   Primula × polyantha
6   Bellis perennis
7   Aquilegia canadensis
8   Tulipa *'Queen of Sheba'*

For flowers later in the season, the bed might be permanently planted with some perennials such as rich red Monarda didyma, *evergreen* Athemis tinctoria *and buff yellow achillea, as well as with annuals such as creamy orange* Celosia *'Apricot Beauty', yellow and orange* Cosmos sulphureus *and French and African marigolds, tawny Mexican sunflower* (Tithonia rotundifolia), *yellow, orange and red nasturtiums and sunflowers, yellow and orange zinnias and the 'Bishop of Llandaff' dahlia which has crimson flowers and bronze foliage.*

RIGHT In a "sunset" border at Giverny, lemon, gold, orange and mahogany wallflowers and deep red columbines are planted in bold brushstrokes beneath standard crab apple trees. The warm colors appear even more intense when they are suffused with the red light of the setting sun. On either side of the long ribbon of wallflowers, sweeps of bearded iris are just starting to break bud, so that as the wallflowers fade, the color from the irises will take their place. The beds beyond the wallflowers are planted in pastel colors – like those of the pink tulips. By placing these pale, cooler colors in the background, an illusion of greater distance is created.

yellow, orange and red that Monet used in his Clos Normand is perhaps best treated as a dramatic seasonal incident. Using plants favored by Monet, try putting 'Orange Emperor' and 'Red Emperor' tulips with yellow 'Carlton' daffodils for a spring scheme that will seem to set the garden ablaze. For summer combine orange and yellow African marigolds with red Ruffles zinnias in front of a mixture of scarlet floribunda roses and orange and yellow nasturtiums. They will seem to grab all the sunlight and hand it right back to you! For autumn use yellow, red and orange dahlias with yellow, red and orange heleniums. Also worth remembering are the plants with vivid autumn berries.

The "sunset" borders that Monet created at Giverny were counterpointed by his planting of cooler, "sunrise", colors at the opposite side of the Grande Allée where they could take advantage of the misty early morning light. Here he used, for example, pink and blue columbines, mauve tulips and pastel pink lupins. Pink and blue are colors that had special appeal to Monet. He painted the stucco of his Giverny house pink (accented with green shutters), and planted pink and blue flowers nearby: pink tulips, peonies and roses to echo the color of the house, and forget-me-nots, blue morning glories and deep blue anchusa to make a contrast. At his Blue House, at the other end of the village, where Monet grew his vegetables, the blue façade, like a sheet of clear blue water, provides a perfect background for pink roses, pearly-pink coral bells *(Heuchera sanguinea)*, rosy-pink valerian *(Centranthus ruber)* and pink shades of towering hollyhocks.

Blue, lavender, cool mauve and pink are restful colors in the garden, especially because flowers in these colors are often pastel. While hot colors will tend to project forward in a landscape, cool colors tend to be recessive, especially when used with touches of white. They can make a confined space seem larger.

The appealing, romantic mood conveyed by cool harmonies is so valued by gardeners that packets containing seeds of blue, mauve and pink varieties of one flower are now easily available, ready to be

LEFT Blue and pink, and also blue, mauve and pink are color schemes favored by Monet and Van Gogh. The appeal in a garden of these cool, harmonious colors is captured by Monet in Agapanthus *(1920). Since there are only blue and white agapanthus in nature, a color effect similar to this one of Monet's could be achieved by using spider flowers.*

RIGHT ABOVE The delicate bi-colored pink and white spider flower (Cleome hassleriana), backlit by the sun so that its outline is a shimmering haze, is seen with blue larkspur in the distance.

RIGHT BELOW A corner of one of the "sunrise" borders in Monet's garden with lavender delphiniums, mauve and white dames's rocket, and pink armeria.

scattered in beds and borders. These include old-fashioned, double-flowered columbines *(Aquilegia vulgaris)*, China asters *(Callistephus chinensis)*, Canterbury bells *(Campanula media)*, larkspur *(Consolida ambigua)*, sweet peas *(Lathyrus odoratus)*, delphiniums, morning glory *(Ipomoea)*, nigella *(N. damascena* Persian Jewels*)*, poppies *(Papaver rhoeas* 'Mother of Pearl'*)*, salvia *(S. viridis,* syn. *S.horminum)*, and campion *(Silene coeli-rosa* Treasure Island Mixed*)*, while wishbone flower *(Torenia fournieri)*, is especially good in shaded locations.

As well as using harmonies and contrasts in color, the Impressionists were acutely aware of the dramatic effect of tonal contrasts – those between light and shade – which are at their most extreme in black and white. Although there are no true black flowers in nature, Decaisne and Naudin identified black and white as a potential scheme for the garden, recommending the use of maroon flowers to represent black ones. Several of Van Gogh's still lifes feature the contrast between the silvery-white seed pods of honesty and deep maroon peonies and hollyhocks. Caillebotte planted an island bed with white, cream, maroon and black pansies at Petit-Gennevilliers – perhaps inspired by the formal beds of "black" *Perilla frutescens* and white pelargoniums that he had seen and painted at his family estate at Yerres. Caillebotte owned one of Monet's most remarkable paintings, *The Magpie* (1869), which shows the black and white bird sitting on a wattle fence in a snow-covered garden. In

ABOVE LEFT *A simple mauve and pink color harmony is produced by combining annual pink mallow* (Lavatera 'Loveliness') *with a mixture of annual* Salvia viridis *which contains violet-blue, pink and mauve in its decorative leaf bracts.*

ABOVE RIGHT *The pale mauve faces of the violas* (V. × wittrockiana) *pick up the paler centers of the bi-colored viola in this vignette of low-growing plants.*

OPPOSITE *This summer profusion of blues, mauves, pinks and whites has resonances of Giverny. Sprawling clumps of catmint, larkspur, campanulas, roses, lavender and* Geranium pratense *are broken up with the frothy white spires of* Reseda alba *and the lacy white flowers of annual Queen Anne's lace* (Ammi majus) *to create a glittering effect.*

LEFT ABOVE *Composed mostly of different varieties of lavender with their hazy silhouettes and silvery foliage, this planting alongside a driveway produces the kind of misty quality that Monet liked to create in his garden.*

LEFT BELOW *The blue, mauve and pink color harmony is enlivened with lacy white flowers to produce a sensation of shimmer in a New Zealand garden designed by Olive Dunn. Some of the important components of this mid-summer extravaganza are: blue lavender, catmint, and perennial geraniums; mauve spires of* Sidalcea *'Rose Queen' and umbels of* Silene armeria; *and pink 'The Fairy' roses and* Erigeron karvinskianus *as edging.*

A COOL COLOR GARDEN (OPPOSITE) *Based on Olive Dunn's garden, shown left, this small garden of about 9×15m (30 × 50 ft) is seen in mid-summer Though the main colors are shades of pink, mauve and blue, the spaces between are liberally planted with foamy white flowers to create a shimmering sensation.*

1   Rosa *'Korona'*
2   Delphinium *'Summer Skies'*
3   Wisteria sinensis
4   Salvia nemorosa
5   Alcea rosea
6   *Gazebo*
7   Cosmos bipinnatus *'Sensation'*
8   Clematis *'Niobe'*

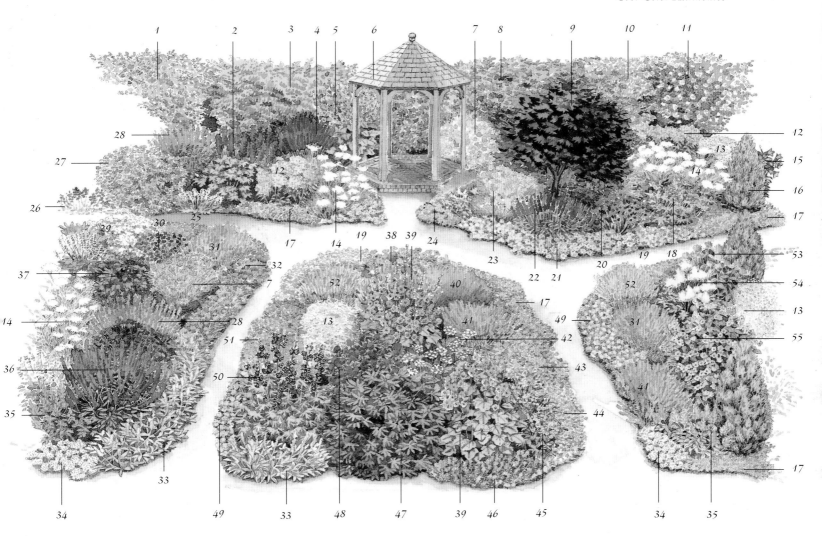

9 Acer palmatum *'Atropurpureum'*	25 Dicentra *'Luxuriant'*	42 Ammi majus
10 Lonicera sempervirens	26 Salvia viridis	43 Geranium *'Johnson's Blue'*
11 Rosa *'New Dawn'*	27 Rosa *'The Fairy'*	44 Geranium sanguineum *var.*
12 Phlox paniculata	28 Lythrum *'Morden's Pink'*	striatum
13 Gypsophila paniculata	29 Salvia *'Rose Queen'*	45 Trachymene coerulea
14 Chrysanthemum parthenium	30 *Cornflowers*	46 Thymus vulgaris
15 Lilium *Pink Perfection*	31 Lavandula *'Munstead'*	47 Rhododendron *pink hybrid*
16 *Dwarf* Chamaecyparis	32 Campanula *'Blue Clips'*	48 Platycodon grandiflorus
17 Lobelia erinus	33 Stachys byzantina	49 Geranium endressii
18 Eryngium × oliverianum	34 Lobularia maritima *'Wonderland'*	50 Sidalcea *'Rose Queen'*
19 Thymus praecox	35 Astilbe × arendsii	51 Geranium himalayense
20 Echinacea purpurea	36 Nepeta *'Six Hills Giant'*	52 Lavandula angustifolia *'Rosea'*
21 Erigeron karvinskianus	37 *Pink Mollis* azalea	53 Thalictrum aquilegiifolium
22 Salvia farinacea *'Victoria'*	38 Petunia *'Pink Joy'*	54 Filipendula vulgaris
23 Monarda *'Croftway Pink'*	39 Lavateria trimestris *'Loveliness'*	55 Lavatera *'Silver Cup'*
24 Lobularia maritima *Summer*	40 Lavandula *'Gray Lady'*	
Pastels	41 Lavandula angustifolia *'Hidcote'*	

homage to this painting, the gardeners at Giverny today use purple-black tulips and black and white pansies to create an unusual black and white vignette.

Other very dark flowers to consider for a black and white scheme are near-black hollyhocks *(Alcea rosea* 'Nigra'*)*; the annual pink that has purplish-black petals tipped with white *(Dianthus chinensis* 'Black and White Minstrels'*)*; the *Nemophila* usually sold as 'Pennie Black'; *Fritillaria persica*, a bulb with dusky-purple bell-shaped flowers; 'Black Velvet' bearded iris; black fountain grass *(Pennisetum alopecuroides* 'Moudry'*)*, and a bamboo with black stems, *Phyllostachys nigra*. Plants with very dark foliage include black mondo grass *(Ophiopogon planiscapus* 'Nigrescens'*)* and a maroon-leaved succulent *Aeonium* 'Schwartkopf'.

On a walk in search of motifs through the countryside outside Arles, Van Gogh encountered a colorful cutting garden planted along a path leading to a farm. The painting, *Flower Garden with Path* (see page 2), is an object lesson in color themes and – remarkably – the garden appears to have been planted in the complementary color combinations Van Gogh had recommended to his sister (see text on pages 43-4) red and green from geraniums and poppies, and yellow and blue from what appear to be yellow zinnias and blue cornflowers. However, the most surprising revelation is a study in orange and black – orange from African marigolds and black from a maroon-colored sweet scabious. Van Gogh expressed his delight at discovering the orange and black color grouping in a letter to his brother, and in a second study, *Flower Garden* (1888), he featured the orange and black combination even more prominently. A third painting of a flower garden, *Flower Garden behind a House* (1888), shows another eyecatching orange and black coupling – this time from orange marigolds and maroon nasturtiums painted black.

At Cedaridge Farm, in mid-summer, an orange and black border honours Van Gogh's revelation. It combines black sweet scabious *(Scabiosa atropurpurea)* and orange marigolds *(Tagetes erecta)*, but also includes orange-petalled black-eyed Susans *(Rudbeckia fulgida).* Yellow and orange annual sunflowers with maroon centers *(Helianthus annuus* 'Fashion Parade' and 'Sunburst'*)* complete the orange and black display which seems to delight visitors more than any other Impressionist planting scheme.

The changing effect of light on color was one of the fundamental tenets of Impressionism. Monet became so obsessed with the changing qualities of light at different times of the day and in different seasons that he would have as many as thirty canvases on the go at one time, switching from one canvas to another after only a few minutes' work, reworking each picture in turn at the same time on subsequent days. In these paintings (the series of *The Thames*, for example) the quality of light

An informal border at Cedaridge Farm echoes the orange and black color theme depicted by Van Gogh in several of his paintings of a garden in Provence. In this-easy-to-grow border, deep claret scabious contrasts with orange marigolds, while the dark centers of annual and perennial rudbeckias and annual sunflowers provide the black accents among the yellow, gold and orange petals.

is translated into pure color. In doing this, Monet was expressing Chevreul's most profound revelation – that colors do not exist except as functions of light; that light alone makes color and defines form. The changing effect of light is also a vital consideration in planning color schemes in the garden. Light reveals colors; it also enhances, dissolves and hides colors, depending on its intensity. For example, bright diffused light – such as from a high overcast sky – can intensify colors and sharpen their visual effect. Conversely, low light levels can dull colors, while glaring sunlight can make bright colors appear washed-out. For this reason, pastel colors in a flower garden tend to look better in partial shade than full sun. White flowers can look sensational in subdued light – even moonlight – while on a bright day large patches of white seem to punch holes in the landscape.

Just as Monet juxtaposed colors on his canvases in small dabs to create the quintessentially Impressionist sensation of "shimmer", so he built up his garden using several techniques to produce a similar sensation. Foremost was his use of broken color, achieved by avoiding big clumps of solid color and scattering lots of white flowers through his borders to add a semblance of sparkle, while also using gauzy white flowers to "veil" other, stronger colors. The use of bi-colored flowers increased the effect of small "strokes" of color (although Monet did not like variegated foliage, finding it sickly in appearance). He preferred

A colony of black and white 'Paramount' pansies and 'Queen of the Night' tulips produce a dramatic color contrast in Monet's garden at Giverny. The contrast of black and white in nature was also admired by Van Gogh and Caillebotte. In the garden it is perhaps best confined to small spaces using just two or three plants together. It is particularly effective as a vignette in a container planting.

single to double-flowered varieties of plants, and loved flowers with translucent or iridescent petals because their light-reflecting qualities increased the cumulative impression of shimmer.

The use of broken color is significant, for it is perhaps one of the main distinctions between Monet's planting philosophy and that of his contemporary across the English Channel, Gertrude Jekyll. Both Monet and Jekyll reacted against the current nineteenth-century fashion for planting in distinct – often geometric – blocks of bright colors, but whereas Jekyll tended to plant in separate drifts of color that dissolved into one another, along her borders, Monet planted his narrow beds in long speckled ribbons of color that stretched the full length of each bed. Jekyll's borders were devised for onlookers to walk along, so that the color and interest changed with the viewpoint; Monet's beds were designed to be painted from a stationary position, the scene needing to be taken in with one glance.

As well as sprinkling white flowers through his garden, Monet planted delicate white flowers in front of bolder masses of blue or pink blooms and dark green foliage. For example, clouds of baby's breath (annual *Gypsophila elegans* or perennial *G. paniculata*) veiled clumps of blue cranesbill *(Geranium himalayense)*; sea lavender *(Limonium latifolium)*

FAR LEFT *A distinctive feature of Monet's House at Argenteuil (1873) is the glimmering effects created by his fluttering brushwork and the small dabs of almost translucent white paint that spangle the whole scene. There are no areas of solid color; everything is built up in small brushstrokes so that the scene seems to shimmer. It was the same effect that Monet was to re-create – with plants instead of paints – at Giverny, using white flowers scattered through his garden.*

LEFT *The airy quality of the pale flowers of chamomile, yellow* Anthemis tinctoria, *creamy feverfew and white* Lychnis coronaria alba *creates a sparkling effect among the darker blues and green foliage in this herb garden made by artist John Hubbard whose work is influenced by Impressionism.*

BELOW *By using the frothy flowers of* Tiarella *and pendants of bluebells as an edging beneath creamy rhododendron blossoms, Princess Greta Sturdza has brought the effect of glimmering light into her woodland garden on the Normandy coast.*

grew in front of a blue clematis; and one contemporary observer noticed "saxifrage (London pride) with light, white blooms and blue wall campanulas *(C. portenschlagiana)*". Other plants whose small white flowers produce a frothy or misty effect range from stately *Crambe cordifolia*, a hardy perennial which grows to 2 metres (6 feet) and meadowsweet *(Filipendula ulmaria)* which Monet used as a foil to the dark foliage in his water garden, to *Gaura lindheimeri* whose 1 metre (3 feet) wand-like stems are covered with flowers resembling butterflies, to low-growing evergreen *Tiarella cordifolia*.

In his sophisticated use of white flowers, Monet may have been aided by Decaisne and Naudin's observations about white in the garden. "All colors, whether primary or compound, are enlivened by the proximity of *white*," they observed. "White has the extra advantage of improving a bad combination by intervening between the colors that go poorly together, as for example, between red and orange, red and purple and purple and blue..."

Flowers with shining petals added to the iridescent quality in Monet's garden: golden and cream-colored California poppies *(Eschscholzia californica)*; orange, white and yellow Iceland poppies *(Papaver nudicaule)*; satin flowers *(Clarkia amoena)* in shell-pink, lavender and white; meadow foam *(Limnanthes douglasii)* with dainty yellow flowers tipped white; single-flowered hollyhocks *(Alcea rosea)* in yellow, apricot, maroon, white and many shades of red; African daisies (especially *Dimorphotheca pluvialis)* in dazzling white, cream, yellow, orange and apricot; and the stupendous single-flowered and semi-double tree peonies *(P. suffruticosa, P. delavayi* and *P.* × *lemoinei)* in shades of white, yellow, pink and red. Mallows such as the purple *Malva sylvestris mauritiana* and hardy hibiscus such as *H. syriacus* 'Blue Bird' with trumpet-shaped blue flowers or *H. s.* 'Diana' with wavy edged white flowers, also have petals that seem to gleam in the light.

Monet loved annual red corn poppies *(Papaver rhoeas)* and large perennial Oriental poppies *(Papaver orientale)* for their translucent quality, planting them freely, but especially where the sun could shine through their petals and make them glow like Chinese lanterns. He also admired Asiatic lilies, sunflowers and cosmos for this extra dimension to their brilliance, and in general preferred single flowers because they

The glimmering sensation created by this mass planting of bi-colored pansies at Cedaridge Farm comes chiefly from the contrast between their pale and dark colors – like the juxtaposition of dabs of different colored paints. Sprinkled through the pansies, to add to the glittering effect, are white flowers – delphiniums, foxgloves, ox-eye daisies and Canterbury bells.

ABOVE LEFT *Clematis were important to Monet; not only did the white* Clematis montana *produce a glittering effect high above his garden when trained along wires and metal supports, but bi-colored varieties added to the shimmering sensation. Today, 'Minuet' provides a particularly attractive contrast with its white and mauve flowers.*

ABOVE RIGHT *The pink flower plumes of annual fountain grass (*Pennisetum setaceum*) and annual* Celosia *'Pink Tassels' both produce the kind of shimmering sensation that Monet pioneered in his Giverny garden.*

OPPOSITE *Modern bi-colored bearded irises grow at Giverny today in a color combination similar to that in Monet's painting on page 40.*

tend to hold their heads up high and transmit light better than doubles.

Of all the plants in Monet's garden, none contributed more to the shimmering effect than the spider flower *(Cleome hasslerana)*, a tender annual from Central America. The spherical flower heads, composed of butterfly-shaped florets with long filaments that project out around the flower, give the plant a spidery appearance. Though the color range includes pink, white, rosy-red, carmine-red and purple in solid colors, it is the white-and-rose bi-color that produces the most beautiful effect. The pure white form is magical as a background highlight, veiling a wall or trellis of vines.

Many of the quivering ribbons of color in Monet's beds included bi-colored flowers such as the lavender and white irises that he depicted in *The Artist's Garden at Giverny* (see page 40). He also favored bi-colored tulips, and *Tulipa* 'Sorbet', a red and white single early tulip, is used in his garden today. *Tulipa* 'Union Jack' and 'Twinkle', which have similar coloring, will also produce a shimmering effect. Other important bi-colored flowers in Monet's plant palette were tuberous dahlias with quilled petals and white tips, and the carmine and white striped *Clematis* 'Nelly Moser'. There are more bi-colored clematis available today including 'Dr Ruppel' which, in addition to its rose-pink and carmine stripes, has a wavy white edging to its sepals.

Not available in Monet's time, but popular with the gardeners who care for Giverny today, are varieties of bi-colored cosmos, significantly

'Daydream' with pale pink petal edges and a deep rosy bulls eye, and 'Candystripe' with pink or white petals and magenta streaks that appear to have been applied with a deft brushstroke. Other bi-colored flowers which, planted in even a small group, will make an oasis of light in the garden include daffodils such as *Narcissus* 'Professor Einstein' which has white outer petals and an orange-red crown, and *N* 'Cragford', a cluster-flowered white and orange Tazetta narcissus used at Giverny today.

Like many of his paintings in which the image is truncated by the frame at the top of the canvas so no sky appears, Monet's garden has flowers high overhead so one's whole sphere of vision is suffused with color. Monet had special metal arches and trellises made to support flowering climbers, such as clematis, morning glories, Cape plumbago *(Plumbago auriculata)*, roses and wisteria. Here, too, he applied similar principles to the skyward planting as he did at ground level, growing two climbers together to provide a mixture of flowers and colors (yellow 'Mermaid' roses and purple Jackmanii clematis, for example), and using white *Clematis montana* to "...form airy garlands with ends free floating in the wind, thus creating an effect like lace curtains", as a visitor described it during Monet's time.

Small flowering trees – such as French lilacs *(Syringa* hybrids*)*, and especially those which produce clouds of blossom such as the pink tamarisk *(Tamarix ramosissima)*, the feathery pink silk tree *(Albizia julibrissin)*, crab apples *(Malus* hybrids*)*, and ornamental cherries *(Prunus* hybrids*)* – also carry color above most of the annuals and perennials at Giverny. The garlands of climbers and strategically placed flowering trees help frame views in the garden, as paintings are defined by carefully chosen frames.

Other good small trees to cultivate for their clouds of blossom include the multi-stemmed, billowing smoke tree *(Cotinus coggygria)* with its airy flower clusters in white, pink and purple, depending on variety; the Judas tree or redbud *(Cercis canadensis)* with masses of rose-pink pea-shaped flowers in spring; and the early flowering *Amelanchier* – especially *A. laevis*, a small multi-stemmed tree form with bronze juvenile foliage and delicate flowers like apple blossom.

That Monet's techniques were as effective in his own time as they are in his restored garden today, we know from the art critic Octave Mirabeau. He has left us with a description of the garden in 1891: "... the hollyhocks dress their masts with exquisite rumpled fabrics, as light and vaporous as gauze, their creases satin-brilliant; they bear little dancer's skirts that balloon and billow ... the dahlias are stars that tremble and twinkle atop fragile branching stems ... [even] the air is filled with so much glimmering, so much quivering ...."

FAR LEFT In Monet's The Lilac Bower *(c. 1872-3) three people sit beneath a canopy of opalescent lilac blossoms. The painting shows several features admired by the Impressionists – a billowing, cloud-like silhouette, sinuous branch patterns and – above all – a glimmering quality produced by the pale, glistening flowers. Monet planted many small trees for the quality of their blossom in his garden at Giverny.*

BELOW An ornamental Japanese cherry (Prunus 'Kwanzan') *at Cedaridge Farm makes a shimmering veil of blossom.*

THE INFLUENCE
OF JAPAN

OPPOSITE The Plum Tree Teahouse at Kameido (c. 1857) by Hiroshige (ABOVE) is one of many Japanese prints that enthralled Van Gogh to such an extent that he made an extremely faithful copy, The Flowering Plum Tree *(1887).*

BELOW This Japanese woodblock print by Hokusai (LEFT), Chrysanthemums and a Honey Bee *(c.1825), is part of a collection belonging to Monet and displayed today in his house at Giverny. Monet also owned Caillebotte's painting (RIGHT)* Clump of Chrysanthemums – Garden at Petit-Gennevilliers *(c.1893). Caillebotte and Monet grew these Japanese plants in their own gardens.*

The late nineteenth-century vogue for "Japonisme" in France not only had a profound effect upon the paintings of the Impressionists, but had a pervasive influence on Monet's creation of a water garden at Giverny. Fascinated by what he knew of Japanese landscaping traditions, he translated these into his own vision of a Japanese stroll garden, using newly imported plants and crowning the effect with the now-famous arched bridge. Monet's water garden differs significantly from what we regard as a Japanese garden today; there are no stone ornaments or radically pruned trees, and no attempt at symbolism. Archive photographs show, however, that in Monet's day, it was closer to the Japanese idiom than it is today with a greater use of soothing, moss-like groundcover plants along the path where there are now clumps of flowers. Indeed, a visiting Japanese diplomat complimented Monet on his interpretation of a Japanese garden.

In 1853, after two centuries of self-imposed isolation, Japan opened its borders to world trade; and by 1862 Japanese arts and artifacts were being sold in specialist shops, and were exhibited at the international exhibitions in London in 1862 and Paris in 1867. A flood of articles

PREVIOUS PAGES Hiroshige's print, Wisteria Blooms over Water at Kameido *(c. 1856) may have influenced Monet in the contruction of the bridge in his Giverny water garden. The crown of Monet's wisteria-covered bridge is a favorite place to pause and admire the pond, its floating islands of waterlilies and rich marginal planting of irises, daylilies and the large, velvety leaves of* Petasites japonicum.

reporting on life in Japan in turn spawned fantasies about Japanese life, such as Pierre Loti's popular novel *Madame Chrysanthème* (on which Giacomo Puccini's opera *Madam Butterfly*, was based) and Gilbert and Sullivan's comic opera, *The Mikado*. Though the most treasured imports from Japan were fabrics, furniture and ceramics, exotic new plants were also eagerly sought. These included the beautiful flowering cherries, such as *Prunus pendula* 'Pendula Rosea' and P. 'Hokusai' introduced by Siebold in the 1860s, and billowing lace-leaf Japanese maples, notably *Acer palmatum* 'Osakazuki', an arrival of 1898. The connoisseur plant collectors among the Impressionists – Caillebotte and Monet – were also captivated by Japanese varieties of chrysanthemums, tree peonies, irises and waterlilies. In a note to Caillebotte sharing a new plant discovery, Monet wrote: "Here is the name of the Japanese plant that I got from Belgium: Cryptochaete. Try to speak to M. Godefroy [a botanist friend] and give me some information on how to grow it".

Of all the imports, woodblock prints on silk and rice paper held the greatest interest for the Impressionists. The Japanese artists used new compositional devices, such as unusual viewpoints – often very high or very low – or heavily truncated subjects in the foreground to frame a view. They showed how colors could be used decoratively and emotionally, rather than purely descriptively; and their subject matter was, to Western eyes, highly unconventional. Traditional European taste admired religious, mythical, historical and didactic themes, where-as Japanese art was rich in scenes from everyday life – including the world of prostitutes and the theater – as well as landscapes and flowers.

Many of the Impressionists collected Japanese prints in large numbers, and Van Gogh organized a successful exhibition in Paris in 1887. One of his reasons for venturing to Provence in the south of France was to seek landscapes like those of Japan. "I believe that by looking at nature under a brighter sky one might gain a truer idea of the Japanese way of feeling and drawing", he wrote. He was not disappointed. "The place, with its clarity of light and the gay effect of its colors seem to be as beautiful as Japan", he declared shortly after his move to Arles.

So great was Van Gogh's enthusiasm for Japan that he felt a psychological affinity to the Japanese, which he expressed in a letter to his sister: "If we study Japanese art, we see a man who is undoubtedly wise, philosophical and intelligent, who spends his time ... studying a single blade of grass. But this blade of grass leads him to draw every plant, and then the seasons, the wide aspects of the countryside, then animals, then the human figure ... isn't it almost a true religion which these simple Japanese teach us, who live in nature as though they themselves are flowers. And you cannot study Japanese art, it seems to me, without becoming much gayer and happier."

Though Monet, in his paintings, drew on Japanese art in a less direct way than other contemporary artists like Degas, Cassatt or Whistler, he held the Japanese aesthetic in high regard. Responding to a magazine writer seeking to understand Monet's art, he asserted: "If you absolutely must find an affiliation for me, select the Japanese of olden times: their rarefied taste has always appealed to me; and I sanction the implications of their aesthetic that evokes a presence by means of a shadow and the whole by means of a fragment."

Like Van Gogh, Monet never visited Japan, but he read about Japanese traditions, art and garden philosophy and welcomed Japanese art patrons to his garden. He crowded the walls of his house with Japanese prints, and he was inspired to copy from one of them an arched wooden footbridge for his garden. He even invited a Japanese horticulturist to Giverny to help him choose appropriate plants.

It was therefore fortuitous that one of the American Impressionist painters who was drawn to Giverny was Lilla Cabot Perry, whose husband's great uncle was Commodore Perry, the naval officer responsible for opening up western trade with Japan. For much of the time between 1889 and 1909 the Perrys lived in Giverny, for a time renting the house next door to Monet (the same one that Butler and Frieseke

LEFT *Monet's Japanese bridge today shows white wisteria veiling the bridge like a lace curtain. Though the white variety comes into full bloom slightly later than the mauve, there is a brief overlap when the mauve and the white mingle their colors.*

ABOVE *Monet, with members of his family and a Japanese visitor, views his water garden from the arched Japanese footbridge in 1921. The winter photograph clearly reveals the construction of the canopy that supports the wisteria.*

would also rent), and Mrs Perry became one of the few foreign artists to develop a close, lasting relationship with Monet, who grew increasingly reclusive and secretive the more he was idolized and sought by art students. In 1897 she accompanied her husband when he accepted a teaching position at a Japanese university in Tokyo. During the ensuing three years she painted prodigiously, depicting Japanese landscapes, gardens, customs, costumes and interiors, and acquired a wealth of knowledge about Japan that would help Monet to interpret the Japanese garden aesthetic better when she returned to Giverny.

In 1893, wishing to extend his garden, Monet had bought a two-acre parcel of land beyond the railway line which formed the lower boundary of the Clos Normand. The plot, a swampy area with some mature willows and birch trees, included a small pond which Monet enlarged – by diverting water from the River Epte – in order to be able to grow waterlilies on its surface. As his knowledge of Japanese garden design

LEFT The Bamboo Garden at Magnolia Plantation, South Carolina, was inspired by Japanese garden design. The footbridge, designed by the author, was influenced by Monet's interpretation of a Japanese bridge. It takes visitors over one of several lakes.

ABOVE The Japanese Bridge (1900) is one of a series of Monet's paintings of his arched bridge before he added the canopy that was to become covered with wisteria.

ABOVE *The path round the pond at Giverny passes a wisteria arbor planted by Monet himself. Bordered by azaleas that enhance the Japanese atmosphere, the path leads to a seat so that visitors may spend time contemplating their surroundings.*

LEFT *Spent azaleas softly carpet a path in this stroll garden, as does the wisteria in Monet's garden. The effect of fallen leaves or petals is a strong element in Japanese garden design; whether Van Gogh knew this or not, he wrote about similar effects made by leaves and pine needles and in Path in the Woods (1887) he shows what might be Judas tree petals strewn along the ground.*

OPPOSITE *Wild plum blossom frames a rustic Japanese-style bridge and exquisite early morning reflections in a pond at Magnolia Plantation, South Carolina. The bankside plantings were planned to enhance the water reflections, as they do in Monet's Giverny water garden.*

and plants increased, so Monet expanded and elaborated the pond, giving it, in 1901, a more pronounced curvature and more luxurious bankside plantings of irises and grasses and, in 1903, adding a canopy of wisteria to the arched bridge.

Monet's close friend, the horticultural expert and writer Georges Truffaut, has left us with a vivid description of the water garden: "On one shore, forming a backdrop, there is a cluster of briary plants among which ferns, kalmia, rhododendrons, and holly predominate ... there are abundant irises of all varieties along the edges of the pond ... Japanese iris ... add an Oriental touch, which is further enhanced by such plants as Japanese tree peonies ... at the water's edge are beds of meadow rue with leaves as lacy as some ferns, with pink and white fluffy flowers. There are also Vanhouttei spiraea with white flowers mingling with tamarisks, whose pink and light blooms are as graceful, in May, as ostrich plumes ... in some corners of the garden are rhododendrons mingling with Chinese and American azaleas in colors ranging from shrimp red to pure white. Long-stemmed rosebushes and bush roses with garlands of blooms forming a frame are everywhere. The overall impression is of a delightful fairyland, one that arouses an ... intense awareness of artistry."

Similar delights await the visitor today. Monet's water garden is reached through an underground passageway built to avoid crossing a busy highway which replaced the old railway line. From the tunnel a

ABOVE LEFT Monet's Waterlilies *(undated but probably from around 1920) shows floating leaves and starburst flowers veiled by the weeping branches of a willow reflected in the water in his garden at Giverny. The same willow frames islands of*

waterlilies today (ABOVE). *In order to maintain its reflective surface, the pond is regularly tended in order to keep it free from weed and to prevent the waterlilies from spreading too far.*

meandering path leads past luxuriant groves of bamboo to the Japanese bridge, at the crest of which is a commanding view of the entire pond. The path leads on through a tunnel of bamboo, skirting the massive trunk of a beech tree with a carpet of moss growing around its roots, past generous plantings of Japanese butterbur *(Petasites japonicus)* to the pond margins where thick clumps of iris – notably the yellow English flag iris *(Iris pseudacorus)* and the blue Japanese water iris *(Iris ensata)* – grow contentedly with their roots permanently submerged in water, while blue lily of the Nile *(Agapanthus africanus)* and tawny daylilies *(Hemerocallis* hybrids) spill their arching sword-like leaves into the water from the dry banks. A token group of tree peonies – the site is now too shady for more than a few plants – represents what was once a much larger collection in white, yellow, apricot, pink, red and maroon, that Monet obtained from Japanese nurseries.

The path then opens out into a sitting area, partly shaded with an arbor of climbing roses, which also serves as a boat dock and observation platform, its stone steps leading down into the water. This vantage point offers a perfect view of several large weeping willows on the opposite bank, their long pendulous branches dipping curtains of slender yellow-green leaves into the water. The path continues over a small green footbridge that crosses a narrow water intake, past bushy rhododendrons planted beneath a grove of indigenous trees. It curves under a wisteria arbor supported as it was in Monet's day, by a rectangular, metal frame, and then, running parallel to what was once the railroad track and is now a road hidden by a high wooden fence trellised with vines, it returns visitors to the Japanese bridge and the tunnel. In spring, the edges of the path are bright with primroses and daffodils; in summer they are flanked with cool pink hydrangeas.

Monet loved to conduct visitors on a personal tour of the water garden, taking them on the route just described. Doing so, he was successfully interpreting the concept of a traditional Japanese Imperial stroll garden, in which emperors would take visiting dignitaries on winding paths around carp ponds. Some of these Japanese stroll gardens, which led from one garden space to another on a visual adventure, were also cup gardens because they featured places designated for introspection. A cup garden can be as big as a mountain lake, the surrounding slopes forming the sides of the cup, or it can be as small as a stone table-top with a bonsai accent in the middle. Thus, in the Japanese idiom, Monet's water garden is a stroll garden within a cup garden – the pond itself forms the bottom of the cup, where the waterlilies and water reflections provide the focus for introspection, and the surrounding greenery of weeping willows, bamboo and thickets of rhododendron form the sides of the cup. The path round the lake

Although it would be possible to add a frame to train wisteria over the bridge, as Monet did, the whole scheme might look too crowded unless the pond was substantially larger. The bridge has been painted "Monet green", and the Oriental-style benches, which are now commercially available in reconstituted stone, are similar to those at Giverny today. A small viewing platform beneath a rose-covered arch recalls Monet's boat dock.

The planting has a Japanese flavor, although a small weeping cherry might be a more practical substitute for the willow which grows tall and fast.

1   Rosa 'Belle Vichysoise'
2   Stone slab viewing platform
3   Iris foliage
4   Hosta seiboldiana
5   Astilbe × arendsii
6   Bamboo
7   Weeping willow
8   Stone bench
9   Petasites japonicus
10 Acer palmatum 'Dissectum Atropurpureum'
11 Paeonia lactiflora
12 Iris pseudacorus
13 Rhododendron hybrid
14 Iris ensata
15 Primula japonica
16 Nymphaea hybrids
17 Carex buchananii
18 Ophiopogon japonicus
19 Paeonia suffruticosa
20 Hemerocallis hybrid
21 Iris laevigata
22 Acer palmatum 'Dissectum Viride'

ABOVE One of the best views of Monet's legendary water garden is from the wisteria-clad bridge. The overall design emulates the concepts of a traditional Japanese cup garden – where the water forms the bottom of the cup and the plantings along the banks its sides, and a stroll garden – where the perimeters are full of incidents to pause and contemplate – both deliberately designed for introspection. Arches of pink Rosa 'Belle Vichysoise' cover the boat dock and viewing platform from where Monet could sit and look at his beloved waterlilies.

A SMALL WATER GARDEN (OPPOSITE) Inspired by Monet's waterlily pond at Giverny, and based on an award-winning design by Stapeley Water Gardens for the Chelsea Flower Show, this pond measures about 18 m (60 ft) in length and is about 12 m (40 ft) at its widest point. The arched wooden bridge, which would have to be made professionally, has a span of about 7.5 m (24 ft) and is about 1 m (3 ft) wide. If the pond was much smaller, the bridge would have to be reduced proportionally, but anything under 60 cm (2 ft) wide would be impractical.

leads to smaller cups including a little moss garden almost completely enclosed by a thicket of bamboo. In the center is a stout beech tree, its bark a beautiful dove-grey and its exposed roots making a decorative contrast to the moss; a semi-circle of three stone benches allows visitors to contemplate the nuances of the scene, and the benches introduce a stone accent so essential to traditional Japanese gardens.

Today, Monet's water garden more closely resembles an English water garden. Originally the color of the marginal planting was more subdued and pale flowers were introduced as oases of light. The emphasis was rather on the difference in shapes, colors and textures of the foliage. In the attention he paid to leaf contrasts, Monet was an innovator; of all his contemporaries, only Gertrude Jekyll, in her writings, shared his concern. Monet edged long stretches of the pond with closely cropped groundcovers of dwarf bamboo and lily turf, and deliberately staged the contrasts between the smooth pointed leaves of bamboo, the velvety round leaves of Japanese butterbur and the leathery, glossy-green leaves of rhododendron hybrids. Further contrasts came from the stiff sword-shaped leaves of water iris, the fountain-like foliage of daylilies, the fan-shaped tree peony leaves and the mounds of feathery maple leaves.

It is not necessary to have a lot of space, or a pond, to create a garden that echoes the Japanese flavor of the stroll garden at Giverny. Even a small garden can be made to seem much larger by threading it with a winding footpath that doubles back on itself in hairpin curves. This

BELOW The interesting leaf shapes and textures in and around this small pool include the blue-green parasol-shaped leaves of a hardy lotus (Nelumbo nucifera), tri-colored Houttuynia cordata 'Chameleon', crinkled leaves of candelabra primula (Primula japonica), spear-shaped leaves of tender water cannas and grass-like leaves of Cyperus papyrus. In the clear water, flat circular leaves of waterlilies contrast with a floating colony of water lettuce (Pistia stratiotes), with enough space in between to allow reflections of the sky. Since most of the plants are tender, they are all grown in pots and overwintered under glass.

should be punctuated by open spaces – in which to pause – that might contain an accent, either a single tree, such as a Japanese maple or a weeping cherry, or a stone accent, such as a basin bench or distinctive boulder, each forming a small cup garden. Hardy bamboo, rhododendrons and camellias will provide evergreen, ornamental leaf shapes and textures, as well as effective screening, while deciduous trees are needed for their spring blossom, autumn colors or winter silhouettes.

To emulate Monet's water garden on a similar scale would be a major undertaking requiring a very large garden, but it is quite feasible to make an amply rewarding one in a far smaller space. Installing a green painted arched bridge would immediately evoke Giverny but, if the proportions are small, it need not be canopied. Even without a bridge, the use of some of Monet's distinctive bankside plantings alone would pay effective homage to his garden. At Cedaridge Farm there is an almost circular pond – with a diameter of 7.5 metres (25 feet) – whose banks are planted, to recall Giverny, with clumps of flag irises, butterbur, varieties of maiden grass *(Miscanthus sinensis)* and *Astilbe × arendsii*. A weeping willow adds an unmistakable note from Giverny, and its foliage is contrasted with that of bushy azaleas, hydrangea hybrids and a weeping cherry *(Prunus pendula* 'Pendula Rosea'). Five of Monet's favorite Marliac waterlilies, grown in black tubs submerged 30 centimetres (12 inches) below the water to make them invisible, form floating islands on the pond. A meandering path circles the pond, crossing the stream that feeds the pond by a small arched bridge.

BELOW CENTER Stones and boulders help to retain mounds of soil around the fringes of a small pond, allowing an assortment of plants grown by Monet, including ornamental grasses and astilbes, to flourish. A group of hardy waterlilies occupies the center of the pond.

BELOW Some of Monet's favorite water margin plants grow beside the pond at Cedaridge Farm. They include a stand of Iris sibirica, *feathery pink astilbes (which Monet knew as spireas) and, on the far bank, a generous clump of butterbur* (Petasites japonicus). *The white fence in the background recalls that enclosing Celia Thaxter's cutting garden, and matches the entrance gate that was inspired by Caillebotte's (see page 120).*

Meadows, Orchards and Woodland

Time and again the Impressionists were drawn to the natural landscape as a subject for their paintings – Renoir joked that he could always recognize an Impressionist painter by his muddy boots, and both he and Van Gogh spoke of being chastised for thoughtlessly tramping into homes with dirty boots after forays into the countryside. However, the Impressionists rarely sought vast, untamed landscapes – with the exception of Cézanne's beloved Mont Sainte-Victoire, and the spectacular Peiroulettes Ravine painted by Van Gogh – but preferred views of the countryside within easy walking distance of towns. Wildflower meadows, dappled woodland and flowering orchards were especially appealing to the Impressionists, some of whom incorporated these into their own gardens.

Few gardeners today have rolling meadows, or acres of woodland, but it is possible to take inspiration from Impressionist paintings, and create natural-looking garden spaces on a small scale – a sweep of poppies or ornamental grasses planted on a sunny bank; a small grove of white birch underplanted with spring-flowering bulbs that readily naturalize; an appealing variety of ivy planted to cloak an unattractive tree trunk; and most people have room for one spring flowering tree for the beauty of its early blossom and the delicate carpet of its fallen petals.

Monet and Renoir loved the wildflowers of Normandy and Provence and painted them repeatedly. Van Gogh, too, was enthralled by the poppies, lavender, thistles and grasses that grew in the warmth of the south of France. Renoir deliberately encouraged native wildflowers and grasses to self-seed beneath the olive and fruit grees in his garden, while Monet sought out the wispy plants, grasses and wildflowers that shimmered in the slightest breeze, calling them "the soul of the garden". He also introduced wild red corn poppies, white ox-eye daisies and bright yellow flag irises into his garden to temper the more contrived look of some of his nursery-bred hybrid peonies and dahlias.

It is not as easy to create a wildflower meadow as one might think. It is a mistake to scatter the seeds like chicken feed and expect them to grow where they fall. Wildflowers cannot usually compete with indigenous weeds and grasses, and they become crowded out before they

PREVIOUS PAGES In his Woman with a Parasol *(c. 1873), which shows knee-deep unmown grass spangled with flowers, Renoir reveals his love of flower meadows and unkempt-looking gardens. (In later years, he would have his own flowery meadow with poppies, ox-eye daisies and wild oat grasses.)*

In a wildflower meadow today the colors of Renoir's painting are echoed in the cornflowers, corn marigolds, corn cockles, poppies and barley stalks .

RIGHT A sheet of pink Shirley poppies and blue cornflowers makes a stunning summer display.

have a chance to germinate. It is better to create islands of bare soil in the meadow and sow seed there in the autumn, so that the plants germinate during cool, wet weather. They can then establish a healthy crown of leaves while there is little or no competition and they will flower the following spring. By keeping the islands of soil relatively weed- and grass-free, wildflowers will reseed themselves.

Renoir painted pastoral scenes, with the wildflowers and shimmering grasses that he loved throughout his life. His taste for natural gardens was formed early in his years living frugally in Montmartre, an area of Paris that contained many overgrown gardens. He rented a small building – a garden folly – in the Rue Cortot and portrayed its unkempt garden in *The Dahlias* (see page 126). Tousled dahlias spill on to an overgrown lawn where a fruit tree sapling seems to struggle for life, while, in the background, his friends Monet and Sisley talk over a lattice fence almost choked with vines. In later years he bought his own garden, Les Collettes, principally for the beauty of its ancient olive trees – which he frequently painted. He would not allow his gardeners to prune the branches too heavily or to cut the native grasses that grew beneath them. One day, when asked permission to weed a path, Renoir asked indignantly, "What weeds?" Though Renoir was crippled with severe rheumatoid arthritis and confined to a wheelchair at Les Collettes, nothing escaped his keen eye. The gardeners needed his approval even to paint or repair shutters, for peeling paint, rusty hinges, and a carefree appearance were all part of his romantic vision of Eden.

Even those Impressionists who had more formal gardens – including Monet and Caillebotte – often portrayed them for romantic effect, making them look more informal and overgrown than they really were. When one looks at Caillebotte's painting, *Sunflowers – Garden at Petit-Gennevilliers* (see page 128), for example, it is hard to believe that the garden itself was based on a highly structured design of geometric-shaped beds and severely pruned rows of fruit trees. Likewise, the highly formal layout of Monet's Clos Normand is not evident in his paintings of it since he chose to paint the garden section by section as each came to the exuberant height of its seasonal planting. Indeed, there is often more inspiration to be gained from the Impressionists' portrayal of gardens than from the gardens themselves.

Trees underplanted with wildflowers, grasses or ivy, or with the ground beneath carpeted with fallen petals or leaves, were favorite subjects of Van Gogh's, and his paintings of *sous bois* include some of the most inspiring ideas for woodland planting. During the two years that he was in Provence in 1888–9, he painted many different olive groves as well as shimmering fields of lavender and poppies. Inspired by these paintings, we have planted a meadow area at Cedaridge Farm

The poppy was painted by the
Impressionists more often than any
other flower – in the meadows of
Normandy by Monet, Cassatt and
Renoir, in Provence by Van Gogh, and
along the cliff tops of Maine by Childe
Hassam.

ABOVE Just as a sweep of annual
field poppies inspired Monet's
painting Wild Poppies (undated),
so the same sense of a wild meadow
can be evoked by a mass planting of
perennial Oriental poppies on a
garden slope (OPPOSITE ABOVE) .

OPPOSITE BELOW Monet planted bright
red poppies and ox-eye daisies among
the more highly bred flowers in his
borders at Giverny. He also planted
Oriental poppies (Papaver orientale)
to make a bold color contrast to stately
bearded irises.

with blood-red flowers of *Papaver commutatum* 'Ladybird' mingled with misty powder-blue flower spikes of 'Munstead' lavender. 'Hidcote' lavender is a deeper blue than 'Munstead', but not so hardy. The poppies are best direct-seeded on to bare soil in late summer and early autumn. They survive even cold winters and will bloom early the following season. Lavender is best propagated from cuttings taken in summer, overwintered in cold frames, and set into their flowering positions in spring.

Other woodland scenes by Van Gogh show shadier plantings. *Undergrowth with Two Figures* (see page 100) depicts a grove of pencil-straight poplar trees against a thicket of dark evergreens, while the grass beneath the poplars is dappled with shadows and white, yellow and orange flowers. At Cedaridge Farm we have planted a grove of twenty four fast-growing river birch (*Betula nigra* 'Heritage') and underplanted them with white, yellow and orange daisies and coreopsis. The lower branches are pruned the better to expose the honey-colored peeling bark. To walk through the airy birch grove with its pale trunks and on into the redwood grove that lies beyond it is to capture the feeling of Van Gogh's painting. Even small gardens can usually find room for a screening grove of five or so trees with decorative bark and an underplanting of shade-tolerant wildflowers.

LEFT Van Gogh's Olive Orchard *(1889) emphasizes the sinuous trunks of olive trees, with blue shadows (which at first glance might be taken for lavender) to complement the strong yellow tones of what appears to be newly scythed grassy undergrowth. A smattering of red poppies gleam at the edges of the cut grass.*

ABOVE LEFT *Beyond the walls of the asylum at Saint-Rémy, Provence, where Van Gogh was an inmate during part of 1888, is a silvery olive grove still underplanted with red poppies. The poppies thrive and reseed themselves in the annually ploughed poor soil.*

ABOVE RIGHT *An olive grove in Provence underplanted with lavender recalls Renoir's olive orchard at Les Collettes. Where the climate is too severe for olive trees, apple or pear trees would make a good substitute. Lavender does demand good drainage and plenty of sun.*

ABOVE *Van Gogh's powerful painting* Undergrowth with Two Figures *(1890) was completed at Auvers, near Paris, just a few weeks before his death. In the garden an equivalent planting of yellow flowers beneath trees could be reinterpreted in many different ways – with spring bulbs, summer annuals or low-growing shade-tolerant shrubs such as azealeas. Van Gogh painted poplar trees, but white birch and the new 'Heritage' river birch would be better choices for smaller gardens. Both display decorative bark which is best revealed by pruning away the lower branches. They have the added advantage of being fast growing.*

It is important to realize that a little extra light can make an enormous improvement in the flowering performance of plants under trees: even the removal of a single branch can be sufficient to make the difference between flowers and no flowers under a tree. Also, there is a great variation between the degrees of shade cast by different trees: the shade cast by an English oak is very dense, while a willow, birch or poplar will cast light, dappled shade. Some good shade-tolerant flowers to consider include bluebells, columbines, daffodils, dame's rocket, daylilies, forget-me-nots, foxgloves, leopard's bane, mimulus, primulas, violets, willow gentians and wood anemones. Plants with evergreen foliage that will put up with shady conditions include hellebores, epimedium, periwinkle, *Pachysandra terminalis* and *Iris foetidissima*.

It is also wise to bear in mind the fact that the area beneath a tree will tend to be dry, as the tree will take up most of the moisture available. If the roots are near the surface, it may be necessary to raise the soil level for other plants by spreading a thick layer of loose, leafy soil over the roots, keeping it away from the tree trunk. It is important to keep the soil well fed and watered.

BELOW LEFT A carpet of hoop petticoat daffodils (Narcissus bulbocodium) has naturalized happily beneath deciduous trees. Since these daffodils need cool, moist summers and are sensitive to severe cold winters, suitable substitutes would be winter aconite (Eranthis hyemalis) and Narcissus asturiensis.

BELOW RIGHT Inspired by Van Gogh's painting, a grove of white birch has been underplanted with annual yellow 'Early Sunrise' coreopsis, annual white 'Silver Princess' Shasta daisies, pink fleabane (Erigeron glaucus), orange-red lychnis (L. × arkwrightii), and lemon daylilies (Hemerocallis citrina).

ABOVE *Van Gogh's* Pine Trees with Dandelions *(1890) shows a pool of ephemeral yellow flowers and silvery seed heads of dandelions in unmown grass around the richly textured trunks of pine trees.*

RIGHT *In quite a different climate, a planting of spring bulbs including blue* Anemone blanda, *white bluebells and small yellow narcissi has been allowed to naturalize beneath an apple tree at the edge of a garden, creating an effect similar in feeling to Van Gogh's painting. Many spring flowers thrive beneath the protection provided by deciduous trees where they benefit from light and sun in the winter and dappled shade in the summer.*

OPPOSITE ABOVE *Van Gogh's* Tree Trunks with Ivy *(1889), painted in the garden of the asylum at Saint-Rémy, shows a grove of pine trees that allows only faintly dappled light to seep through to the undergrowth. Ivy is one of the few plants able to survive the dense, dry shade beneath evergreen trees.*

OPPOSITE BELOW *The ivy (Hedera helix) that has been allowed to girdle this pine tree grows through a thick carpet of evergreen Japanese spurge (Pachysandra terminalis). Outside the leaf canopy is a pool of pale mossy green lawn that echoes the light beyond the group of pine trees in Van Gogh's painting.*

One of the woodland features that seems to have been consistently admired by the Impressionists was an arbor of trees, the path beneath criss-crossed with shadows, and the branches sometimes meeting overhead to make a tunnel of leaves. Whether formed by a specially planted avenue of sycamores – as at Cézanne's family home, Jas de Bouffan – or by the natural growth of an ancient copse of olives, shady canopies and leaf tunnels appealed particularly to Cézanne and Renoir who painted them and cultivated them in their gardens. The dominating effect today in the gardens that surround Cézanne's studio, Les Lauves, is of winding paths enveloped by the arching branches of trees and arborized shrubs.

Among the trees and shrubs in Cézanne's garden are many that

FAR LEFT Cézanne's painting, Road to Mas Jolie at the Château Noir *(1895-1900), shows shadow patterns beneath a luxurious canopy of foliage. Cézanne tried to buy the Château Noir, near Aix-en-Provence, after he had sold his family home and though unsuccessful, he rented a room there in order to store some of his paintings.*

LEFT Cézanne often painted the old stone walls that formed the boundaries of farms and fields beyond the walls of his studio at Les Lauves. By using the rough Provençal stone for his terrace and steps, he brought the flavor of the countryside into his garden. Here rustic steps ascend a slope towards one of the leaf tunnels that winds through the garden.

BELOW Judas trees or redbuds (Cercis canadensis) *line a gravel path, their branches forming a leaf tunnel. The path is edged with shade-loving hostas which in summer have erect flower stems, as tall as foxgloves, studded with white, lavender-blue or purple flowers. In autumn many of the hosta leaves change color to echo the golden yellow and parchment brown of the turning Judas tree foliage.*

flower. A horse chestnut *(Aesculus hippocastanum)*, with its large, serrated many-fingered leaves, covers itself in white "candle" flowers in early summer; a Judas tree produces clouds of its pink flowers on bare stems before the heart-shaped leaves appear; and mock oranges *(Philadelphus)* provide a mass of fragrant white flowers in summer.

The shapes and colors of trees themselves held a fascination for Van Gogh, and his letters are filled with references to the particular tree shapes he admired during walks in the countryside and in public parks. In his studies of a garden that had been owned by Charles F. Daubigny, a *plein air* artist he admired, it is the foliage effects of surrounding trees that dominate. Also, in one of several paintings he made of Dr Gachet's garden he concentrated on the spiky blue-green yucca leaves, a column of dark green juniper foliage, the yellow-green top-knot of a tree-form rose, and bright green clump-forming grasses.

After painting a particularly eye-catching group of trees and shrubs in a park outside his lodgings in Arles, *The Garden of the Poets* (1888), Van Gogh described the concept of what is known today as a "tapestry garden", in which silhouettes combine with foliage hues and textures to create a panorama of subtle color harmonies and contrasts.

BELOW Seeing the shapes and colors of the trees in a public park in Arles in late September inspired Van Gogh to paint The Garden of the Poets *(1888).*

OPPOSITE This predominantly green garden presents a subtle tapestry of foliage colors, textures and contrasting tree shapes. The evergreens include cone-shaped Alberta spruce, blue spire-like 'Skyrocket' junipers, cushion-shaped evergreen azaleas and prostrate ivy. As autumn advances many of the deciduous trees, which include maples and ginkgo, will turn russet colors, creating a more dramatic contrast with the needle- and broadleaf evergreens.

Among the many broadleaf trees and shrubs with unusual shapes and colors suitable for small gardens are *Aucuba japonica*, with shiny evergreen leaves, bronze-leaved *Berberis thunbergii atropurpurea*, the silvery Russian olive *(Elaeagnus angustifolia)*, the corkscrew willow *(Salix matsudana* 'Tortuosa') and the weeping birch *(Betula pendula)*. To make a good tapestry effect, they are best mixed with needleleaf conifers which come in any number of shapes and sizes from slender fastigiate columns to prostrate spreading domes in blue, gold or green.

Autumn color particularly appealed to Van Gogh as well as to Sisley and Monet. In Monet's *Poplars* series (1891) tall trees with buttery yellow leaves and pink-tinted trunks stand out against a pale blue sky, while Van Gogh's series *Les Alychamps* (1888) emphasizes a golden carpet of fallen leaves. These images teach us that trees can be considered not only for skyline beauty, but also for exotic carpeting effects. The spent blossoms of ornamental cherries, for example, briefly color the ground like confetti in spring; and the richly hued autumn leaves of trees such as maples make colorful, ephemeral carpets when they drop to the ground, before being swept up and relegated to the compost heap.

A TAPESTRY OF SCREENING TREES
This grove of trees was inspired by Van Gogh's Garden of the Poets.
1 Cedrus atlantica *'Glauca Pendula'*
2 Ginkgo biloba *(male form)*
3 Picea glauca *var.* albertiana *'Conica'*
4 Ilex × meserveae *'Blue Angel'*
5 Tsuga canadensis *'Pendula'*
6 Picea pungens *'Montgomery'*
7 Juniperus procumbens *'Nana'*
8 Acer palmatum *'Dissectum Viride'*
9 Acer palmatum *'Dissectum Atropurpureum'*
10 Sagina subulata *'Aurea'*
11 Juniperus horizontalis *'Wiltonii'*
12 Corylus avellana *'Contorta'*
13 Betula papyrifera
14 Juniperus chinensis *'Blue Alps'*
15 Chamaecyparis pisifera *'Sungold'*

RIGHT At Le Vasterival, on the Normandy coast, an almost black-green Serbian spruce echoes the spruce in Van Gogh's painting, The Garden of the Poets. Beyond, the mint-greens of deciduous trees make a clean background for drifts of more exotic leaf colors – purple from a Japanese maple, apricot from sycamores, silvery-blue from a willow-leaf pear – while a lower storey of flowering shrubs adds orange from an Exbury azalea, and yellow from a Spanish broom.

BELOW The sumptuous tapestry of foliage in this garden at Titoki Point in New Zealand comes from plants that are also found in the Impressionists' gardens: spiky New Zealand flax borders the terrace of Renoir's garden, fleece-like Japanese Hakonechloa grass borders paths in Cézanne's garden, while heart-shaped blue hostas and billowing Japanese maples surround the pond in Monet's garden.

The glorious sight of orchards in bloom captivated the Impressionists, and lifted the spirits of Van Gogh when he visited Provence. Following a warm spell that forced apricot, plum, peaches, pears and apple trees into bloom, Van Gogh bubbled with enthusiasm in a letter to his brother: "I am up to my ears in work, for the trees are in blossom and I want to paint a Provençal orchard of astounding gaiety." (Interestingly, Van Gogh's portrayal of the orchards is so accurate that pruning expert Robert Gutowski, at Philadelphia's Morris Arboretum, Pennsylvania, uses slides of Van Gogh's fruit tree paintings to teach pruning methods.)

Monet, Sisley and Pissarro all made memorable images of country orchards in spring. Monet so valued the quality of early blossom that, although he consigned all other fruit and vegetables to a separate kitchen garden along the road when he bought the house at Giverny, he replaced the diseased or dying fruit trees in his Clos Normand garden with new apple and pear trees, which were trained as espaliers, and planted ornamental crab apple and cherry trees.

RIGHT Monet's Spring (1886), shows two figures seated beneath plum trees in bloom, the flower petals glittering in the sky above.

ABOVE In Ruth Levitan's Connecticut garden flowering dogwood (Cornus florida) trees carry blossom high into the sky. Pink bleeding hearts (Dicentra spectabilis) and azaleas create a floral understorey, while blue forget-me-nots and blue sweet violets spangle the woodland floor.

A full-blown fruit orchard is not within the scope of many home gardens today, but there are ways in a comparatively small space to enjoy the blizzard of flowers that so appealed to the Impressionists: by using some of Caillebotte's fruit training techniques – especially espalier and fan training against a wall, and low cordon training to define a sunny lawn or flower bed (see page 35); and by using dwarf varieties of fruit trees. Some varieties of peaches and nectarines are so compact in their growth habits they can be grown in a tub on a patio. Many varieties of apples and pears have been dwarfed by grafting onto a special dwarfing rootstock and can be used as a small tree accent in the centre of a flower bed; one must take care to determine if the trees are self-pollinating.

Some of the best spring flowering trees for small gardens include ornamental crab apples (*Malus* hybrids) and cherries (*Prunus* hybrids). Among the best cultivars are disease-resistant *Malus* × *schiedeckeri* 'Red Jade', a weeping crab apple with rosy pink blossom and dark red fruit, which grows at Giverny today, and *Malus* 'Katherine', a standard tree with pale pink flowers and bright red fruit.

Van Gogh, Renoir, Monet and Cézanne admired the effect of uncut grasses, especially when they were allowed to form fountain-like clumps with decorative seed heads that rustle in the wind, their slender arching leaves flashing silver and gold. In Cézanne's garden today, tufts of glossy dark-green Japanese *Hakonechloa* grass edges rustic paths, and silver-spiked fountain grass *(Pennisetum alopecuroides)* cascades from

ABOVE Van Gogh, like Renoir and Sisley, strove to capture the effect of the wind blustering through trees or long grass. In his Wheat Field with Lark (1887) *the ripe grain stalks are bending beneath the breeze.*

LEFT Miscanthus transmorrisonensis *spills its golden seed heads into a driveway. In the foreground are the stiffer flowering stems of* Pennisetum alopecuroides *'Moudry'.*

terracotta urns, its graceful blades contrasting with the velvety, ivy-shaped leaves of trailing and scented-leaf geraniums. At Les Collettes, wild oat grasses are still allowed to form tall, vigorous golden-hued clumps crowned with feathery seed heads; and around the walls of the asylum at Saint-Rémy there are still clumps of the sedge grasses and blue oat grasses that were painted by Van Gogh, the spaces between them bright with wild pink-flowered thyme and yellow-flowered spurge. Monet painted grassy clumps bordering his garden at Giverny, and today bamboo and Japanese miscanthus grasses are still important components of his restored water garden.

Ornamental grasses are mostly carefree and drought-tolerant and can be used either to create a small-scale grass garden in a bed on their own, or they can be combined with flowering annuals and perennials. An assortment of ornamental grasses can also be easily grown in pots on a terrace. In addition to bright green grasses exhibiting different leaf formations, there are yellow, blue, silver, bronze and even a brilliant red, known as Japanese blood grass *(Imperata cylindrica)*. Grasses can also be selected for interesting autumn colors: *Miscanthus sinensis* var. *purpurascens* turns red and purple, and varieties of *Pennisetum* produce colorful seed heads in silver, red, pink, white and a spectacular near-black *(Pennisetum alopecuroides* 'Moudry'). At Cedaridge Farm the grass garden displays a diversity of colors which changes subtly through the year, and only needs cutting back when new grass appears in the spring.

RIGHT *Tinted silver by hoar frost and the cool, misty light of early morning, the grasses beside a stream at Cedaridge Farm include tall striped eulalia grass* (Miscanthus sinensis 'Variegatus'), *amber fountain grass* (Pennisetum alopecuroides), *wisps of Japanese blood grass* (Imperata cylindrica), *low-growing clumps of blue fescue* (Festuca glauca), *and brown New Zealand sedge grass* (Carex buchananii).

ORNAMENTATION

The Impressionists found their subjects in functional garden items, such as trellised arbors, slatted wooden benches and metal watering cans, as well as in colorful planting schemes. Many of the garden structures and furnishings that appealed to them were in vogue at the time and are recurring themes in their work. Versailles tubs, for example, appear in the paintings of Monet, Caillebotte and Van Gogh, and green painted benches in those by Manet, Monet, Renoir, Caillebotte and Van Gogh. Some of the Impressionists created their own embellishments for the garden. Caillebotte designed a distinctive white garden gate, for instance and, on a far grander scale, Renoir created a magnificent bronze sculpture, *Venus Victrix*, to stand on a brick pedestal as a stupendous centerpiece for his garden at Les Collettes. He even planned a Florentine water garden with ruined columns to surround her, though he died before this could be executed.

The master of garden structures among the Impressionists, however, was Monet. For his garden at Giverny he created features that were both practical as well as decorative in themselves, notably the arched

PREVIOUS PAGES Childe Hassam's The Garden in its Glory *(1892) features the simple arch that led from Celia Thaxter's cutting garden to her clapboard house. Red hollyhocks, red poppies and yellow coreopsis gleam among the greenery. Similar metal arches frame the view to the front door of a New England house today.*

ABOVE Monet beneath his rose-covered boat dock at Giverny during the last summer of his life in 1926.

RIGHT A cascade of Rosa *'Albertine' over a garden seat recalls Monet's* The Lilac Bower *(see page 74).*

OPPOSITE ABOVE Monet often planted two flowering climbers together so that they entwined like threads of fabric. Here the climbing rose 'America' is host to Clematis 'Venosa Violacea'.

OPPOSITE BELOW These arches supporting 'American Pillar' roses are similar to those that lead to Monet's boat dock.

Japanese bridge and the Grande Allée of six metal-framed, rose-covered arches. They also became the subject of a series of his paintings.

In addition to the six pairs of metal arches that form the central rose avenue of the Clos Normand, Monet installed arches to cover his boat dock with roses in the water garden. He also designed rectangular metal supports to "frame" the beds in the flower garden. The uprights supported a variety of climbers, while the horizontal spans overhead were festooned with plants with lacy white flowers, including the star-like blooms of *Clematis montana* and fleecy *Fallopia baldschuanica* (syn. *Polygonum aubertii)*. Both contributed to the sensation of shimmer that was a distinctive feature of the garden. For the modern gardener all Monet's metal frames could be happily adapted to smaller gardens, and many pre-formed shapes and sizes are commercially available from garden centers and mail order sources, and are easy to install.

Trelliswork is seen in several Impressionist paintings, particularly in those by Manet and Monet. Trellis not only provides support for climbing plants, but will cast interesting patterns of light and shade.

ABOVE *Monet's* The Luncheon *(c.1873) shows his garden at Argenteuil and features several of his favorite elements of garden design – strong shadow patterns cast by the canopy of branches, flower beds planted in a complementary color scheme of red and green, plenty of frothy white flowers to add a shimmering sensation, a planter, and a slatted wooden bench.*

OPPOSITE *All three of these benches appear either in the gardens or the paintings of the Impressionists. The four-seater wooden bench with metal legs (BELOW LEFT) is very similar to that shown in Manet's painting on page 50. Here it occupies a corner of Les Moutiers, at Varangeville, in Normandy – a garden created during the Impressionist era, close to a section*

of cliffs where Monet painted forty-four canvases of the coast. The green slatted bench (BELOW RIGHT) is seen in many of Monet's paintings, and is still in production today. The group of six-seater curved benches (ABOVE RIGHT), painted the distinctive "Giverny" green, stand in a semi-circle beneath the shade of a Paulownia tree in Monet's flower garden.

It can be used to form arbors and arches, to break up monotonous stretches of wall and to make decorative divisions between areas of the garden. It can be bought or made up into a variety of designs and stained or painted to match other garden features, as shown in Manet's *The Bench* (see page 50) and seen at Giverny today.

The garden furniture most often featured by the Impressionist painters was benches, usually painted green. Monet's garden today is full of wooden benches painted to match the shutters of his house. Most are conventional seats with squared-off corners and a flat rectangular back. More distinctive are the group of three curved benches based on one that Monet spotted in a cottage garden in the grounds of Versailles Palace. These are unusually large and will accomodate six people with ease. The couturier Yves Saint Laurent so admired these benches at Giverny that he had several copies made for his own garden, the Château Gabriel, in Normandy.

In his water garden, however, Monet used three curved Oriental stone benches, grouped in a semi-circle, surrounded by bamboo. Van Gogh, too, was drawn to the stone seats that he encountered in the gardens at Saint-Rémy. These seats, which are still in place today at the asylum, are massive blocks of limestone, supported by smaller slabs, hewn from an ancient local quarry.

Of the containers used for potted plants at the time, the classic wooden Versailles tub was probably the most popular. Monet used them on his terrace at Argenteuil for fuchsias, and Caillebotte's family used them for citrus trees that needed to be brought inside during the

winter. Monet also used his blue and white Oriental ceramic pots as accents in all his gardens at Vétheuil, Argenteuil and Giverny, planting them with gladiolus, sunflowers and white marguerites. Cézanne and Renoir both used terracotta pots for displays of geraniums along their terraces, and Italian olive jars are filled with trailing ivy-leaf geraniums at Les Collettes today.

Gardener's tools such as scythes and sickles, orchard ladders, chunky wooden wheelbarrows and glass bell jars feature in Impressionist paintings. Although these have now been superseded by lighter weight, more efficient or mechanized tools, old implements – if you can pick them up in flea markets or junk stalls – can be displayed for ornamental rather than practical use, to add an Impressionist period flavor.

RIGHT Caillebotte's painting The Artist's House at Petit-Gennevilliers *(c.1882) shows a strong axis along the north fence in perfect alignment with the church steeple at Argenteuil, on the opposite bank of the River Seine. The criss-cross gate, at the entrance to the garden, was the artist's own design. The same pattern has been used by the author at the entrance to Cedaridge Farm (ABOVE).*

LEFT *Morisot's* The Cherry Tree *(1891) shows two women using an A-frame orchard ladder to pick the fruit. Similar ladders feature in other Impressionist paintings, including those of Van Gogh portraying women harvesting olives in Provence. The A-frame ladder that leans against an old pear tree in the author's garden at Cedaridge Farm (BELOW) is used for purely ornamental effect. It makes a particularly strong statement in winter snow, when its straight lines contrast appealingly with the jumble of fruit tree branches and arching canes of a forsythia hedge.*

FAVORITE FLOWERS

PREVIOUS PAGES Van Gogh's Poppies in a Vase *(1888) was an experiment in pairing opposites in color, "seeking... to harmonize brutal extremes... trying to render intense color and not a grey harmony." Here he uses vivid red poppies against an intense blue background. Shirley poppies* (Papaver rhoeas) *have been developed from the European corn poppies* (Papaver commutatum) *that Van Gogh painted.*

The Impressionists not only painted plants growing outside, but also cut them to bring indoors as subjects for still lifes. Of all the different plants portrayed by the painters, a few stand out as their favorites. Certain flowers have come to be associated with particular artists – waterlilies with Monet, sunflowers with Van Gogh, chrysanthemums with Caillebotte and roses with Renoir. These and other flowers, such as poppies, appear repeatedly in the painters' work – many depicted in surprising detail. Perhaps this is because once the flowers were brought into the studio, they were far less subject to the ever-changing light of the open air so that the painters were better able to concentrate on the petal shapes and foliage textures.

Alcea rosea (HOLLYHOCK)

Native to China and Japan, these hardy biennials were admired by the Impressionists for their spire-like growth, deeply-lobed green leaves and their satiny, cup-shaped flowers that hug the upper flower stem. Monet grew them at Giverny and also had them earlier in his rented garden at Argenteuil. His notebook for 1872–5 lists seven rows in purple, white, red, violet, yellow, cream and pink. Though Van Gogh and Frieseke both painted double-flowered hollyhocks (Van Gogh in arrangements), Monet preferred to grow the old-fashioned single-flowered varieties because of the iridescent quality of their blooms. Hollyhocks look their best when they are planted along a picket fence, against brick or stone walls, and beside other garden structures, such as tool sheds and gazebos. In an exposed position, they may need staking to prevent wind damage. They prefer a sunny location and will survive in poor soils, providing drainage is good. They tolerate coastal situations (which is where Childe Hassam captured their stately beauty in Celia Thaxter's garden). Recent plant breeding advances have produced annual types that are resistant to hollyhock rust disease, and they will flower the first year from seed started eight weeks before outdoor planting.

LEFT *Frieseke* Hollyhocks *(c.1914)*

RIGHT ABOVE *Caillebotte* White and Yellow Chrysanthemums *(c.1893)*

Chrysanthemum

The chrysanthemum that the Impressionists liked to paint most in arrangements was the autumn-flowering kind from Japan, which they had seen depicted in so many lively compositions in Japanese prints. Caillebotte had a large collection of Japanese chrysanthemums in his garden at Petit-Gennevilliers, where he grew those with heavy, round, tousled heads, commonly called "football" mums. His painting, *Clump of Chrysanthemums* (see page 78), shows a group in chiefly russet tones in a corner of his garden.

They are so highly evocative of autumn, you can almost smell a touch of frost in the air. Half-hardy perennials, the Japanese chrysanthemums come into bloom when the days shorten in autumn, although modern plant breeders have now developed kinds which will bloom in spring and summer. The large "football" type needs to be lifted and stored in a frost-free place during the winter but the smaller-flowered varieties, which Monet grew and painted, are fully hardy. They prefer a sunny site and well drained soil, and can be propagated by cuttings taken in the spring.

Dahlia

Both Renoir and Monet admired the bedding-type of dahlias that can be grown from seed as annuals, as well as the more flamboyant tuberous dahlias that can grow to 1.8 m (6 ft) in height, with individual flowers up to 25 cm (10 in) across. The color range is extensive – white, yellow, orange, purple, crimson, pink, and bi-colors that include the crimson edged in gold, and the white with

ABOVE Dahlia *'Bishop of Landaff'*

LEFT Renoir The Dahlias – Garden in the Rue Cortot *(1876)*

pink and yellow petal tips that Monet grew. A tall, daisy-flowered red cultivar, 'Bishop of Llandaff', has wonderful bronze foliage and was a favorite of Celia Thaxter and of Monet. Like gladiolus, the tuberous kinds should be planted after the danger of frosts has passed in spring. Though they are "everblooming", producing flowers until autumn frosts, the autumn display may dwindle unless successive plantings are made with the tubers, up to mid-summer. Natives of Mexico, dahlias flower best when nights are cool, prefer full sun or light shade and a soil that drains well. Dahlias have brittle, hollow stems, and soon wilt after cutting unless immediately plunged in water. For longest-lasting display, cut in the cool of the day and place in a cool sheltered area for 4 – 6 hours before arranging.

Gladiolus

Both Van Gogh and Renoir painted still lifes of gladiolus, and Monet loved them in the garden, for they produced vertical accents, like exclamation marks. Developed from a species native to Africa, these tender perennials grow from bulbous corms, and have slender, stiff, sword-like leaves and tall flower spikes studded with ruffled, flared flowers that are mostly portrayed as red or pink in Impressionist paintings, but which also come in white, yellow, orange, purple and green, as well as in bi-colors. They need a sunny, fertile, well-drained site and will flower from mid-summer to autumn if planting of the corms is staggered at two-week intervals after frost danger in spring. In areas where the ground freezes, gladioli can be lifted in autumn and stored in a frost-free area for replanting the following spring. The plants usually need staking to keep them erect, although a planting of bushy annuals – such as African marigolds – around their flower stems can often provide sufficient support. They make excellent, long-lasting cut flowers.

Van Gogh Vase with Gladioli *(1886)*

Caillebotte Sunflowers – Garden at Petit-Gennevilliers *(c.1885)*

Helianthus annuus (*SUNFLOWER*)

Native to North America, this tender annual relishes hot, sunny summers. Van Gogh found both single- and double-flowered varieties growing profusely in the south of France after moving there from Paris in search of new motifs. "You know the peony is Jeannin's, the hollyhock belongs to Quost, but the sunflower is mine ...", wrote Van Gogh to his brother, Theo. He feverishly painted sunflowers to decorate his room in the Yellow House at Arles before Gauguin came to visit him in 1889. During that visit Gauguin did a portrait of Van Gogh showing him intently painting an arrangement of double-flowered sunflowers. The dwarf 'Teddy Bear', which forms a compact bushy plant about 1.2 m (4 ft) high, most closely resembles Van Gogh's double-flowered sunflowers. Some of Monet's paintings of his garden at Vétheuil feature tall, giant-flowered sunflowers similar to those painted by Caillebotte in his garden at Petit-Gennevilliers, and by Pissarro in his at Eragny. Today these are sold as 'Mammoth Russian'. Sunflowers resent transplanting and are best grown from seed sown directly into the garden after frost danger in spring. They need fertile, clay or loam soil, and the species will grow up to 3 m (10 ft). After flowering, the flower centers develop heavy heads of edible seeds. The swirling pattern formed by the dried heads without petals so fascinated Van Gogh that he painted them.

Iris

Bearded irises were developed from a species of iris native to Europe and Asia. Hardy perennials, they produce a clump of swollen roots called rhizomes, from which emerge handsome, blue-green, sword-shaped leaves and a complex flower composed of one set of petals that arches up and a second set that falls down. A woolly cluster at the center of the flower forms the "beard". Van Gogh painted blue bearded irises, both growing in large clumps and as cut flowers in vases, as a symbol of the south of France. In Renoir's garden there is an undulating bed of lavender-colored irises that extends for more than 25 m (80 ft) down a slope. Monet planted, and then painted the glorious effect of, swathes of pale lavender and purple iris in parallel borders at Giverny. He also grew every color mutation he could lay his hands on, especially bi-colored kinds with white upper petals to produce the shimmering effect he liked. The full range of iris colors is so extensive that collections of 6,000 varieties are known today. Propagated by division of the rhizomes after they have flowered, bearded iris need a sunny, well drained location so that the rhizomes can be baked by the sun, and a sandy loam soil rich in phosphorus. Though the flowering season is short, the sight of a full border in bloom is sensational. Indoors – and after rain – they pervade the air with a peppery fragrance. The irises most often depicted in Japanese prints are a species of water iris *(I. ensata)* and the Siberian iris *(I. sibirica)*, both available in blue, deep purple and white. The European flag iris *(I. pseudacorus)* is usually yellow. The edges of Monet's pond at Giverny are planted with generous clumps of all three of these species. They all tolerate their roots permanently submerged in shallow water, and are suitable for cutting.

Irises growing in Renoir's garden

Lilium (ASIATIC AND FAR EASTERN LILIES)

These exotic, yet hardy lilies, which grow from bulbs, were a favorite of Monet, who planted them in the beds throughout his Clos Normand garden and in pots close to the house, while white trumpet lilies *(L. longiflorum)* are seen in Celia Thaxter's garden, painted by Hassam. *L. regale*, introduced in the early years of this century, justifiably remains one of the most popular summer-flowering white lilies. Asiatic and Far Eastern lilies, such as hybrids of *L. auratum,* produce tall flower stems topped with clusters of large, nodding, fragrant flowers –

usually white with a yellow stripe, the waxy petals elegantly reflexed and spotted towards the center. Asiatic and Far Eastern lilies today are mostly hybrids because the species tend to be disease-prone and short-lived. The scaly bulbs are best planted in the autumn or early spring into a humus-rich, fertile, well-drained soil in sun or partial shade. They generally need staking. In cold winter climates the planting site benefits from a covering of shredded leaves after the ground has been frozen, to prevent premature thawing, which can rot the bulbs.

ABOVE Frieseke Lilies *(undated)*   *ABOVE RIGHT* Lilium regale *Album Group*

Nymphaea (WATERLILY)

Monet's waterlilies are perhaps the most celebrated of all his flowers, immortalized in his series of *Nymphéas* paintings. Though waterlilies are not commonly seen as cut flowers, they can be cut and brought inside as a subject for still lifes. Most arrangers like to float them in a bowl, but Childe Hassam painted them in Celia Thaxter's parlor atop tall, slender fluted vases. The waterlilies Monet liked above all others were developed in the south of France by Joseph Bory Latour-Marliac who had a nursery south of Bordeaux in the village of Temple-sur-Lot. Here he collected all the known hardy waterlily species: *Nymphaea alba*, the European white pond lily; *N. odorata*, a fragrant white from North America which included a pink

form found on Cape Cod; and *N. odorata*, a yellow from Central America. There was no hardy red, but Marliac discovered a variety of *N. alba* known as var. *rubra* on Swedish lakes. It opened pink and turned deep red at maturity. With this gene pool Marliac developed a new race of hardy waterlily hybrids. His work produced more than sixty cultivars, most of which Monet grew in his water garden. Known as *N. × marliacea*, many are top sellers among waterlily enthusiasts today, including 'Marliacea Rosea' (pale pink), 'Escarboucle' (rich carmine-rose), 'Colossea' (huge fragrant white) and the remarkable 'Gloire de Temple-sur-Lot' (pink, with 100 curled petals that give it a ball shape, more like a football chrysanthemum). Marliac kept no records of his breeding work, but at a lecture to The Royal Horticultural Society, London, in 1898, he claimed to have used pollen from certain tropical night-blooming species. The resulting hybrids, he said, inherited from their male parent the richest shades of color; and from the female side, not only hardiness, but their ability to bloom in the day. However, experts today believe that there is not a trace of tropical species in any of them. Waterlilies are aquatic perennials and need their tuberous roots permanently submerged in water. They are best planted in sunken containers with a covering of protective wire mesh. They like a fertile clay loam and a cover of 30–60 cm (1–2 ft) of water.

LEFT Monet Waterlilies – Green Reflections *(undated)*

ABOVE *Waterlilies on Monet's pond*

Paeonia (PEONY)

Herbaceous peonies are mostly varieties of *P. lactiflora*, a native of Tibet, China and Siberia. The flowers are showy, often highly fragrant, and valued for their long life after cutting. *P. lactiflora* 'Festiva Maxima', a double white flecked with crimson, was popular in the era of the Impressionists and seems to be the one painted by Renoir in his early still life (see below). Monet grew masses of herbaceous peonies and was so interested in discovering the latest and best hybrids that he traveled to England to visit the nurseries where they were being bred. His painting *Peonies* (1887) shows rows of them shoulder-to-shoulder, their flowers like scoops of pink ice cream. Today there are white, red, deep pink, pale powdery pink and bi-colored herbaceous peonies growing in the Clos Normand at Giverny.

Tree peonies (mostly *P. suffruticosa*) are generally native to mountainous regions of China though Monet referred to them as Japanese peonies. They develop woody stems and usually have larger flowers and are much bushier and taller than their soft-stemmed cousins. Their color range includes maroon, yellow

Renoir Spring Bouquet (1866) includes peonies, irises, wallflowers, lilac and laburnum.

and apricot. Monet concentrated a fine collection of rare tree peonies in a circular bed near the pond in his water garden. Tree peonies can be grown in areas with mild winter climates, whereas herbaceous peonies need a sharp cold spell in winter to flourish. Both herbaceous and tree peonies can be single and double-flowered, and generally they require staking to keep the heavy flower heads erect. They need a fertile, humus-rich soil and the herbaceous sorts are best planted from sections of tuberous roots containing several fat growing points. Planted in autumn, peonies will generally bloom in spring to early summer, the tree peonies several weeks before the *P. lactiflora* cultivars.

Rose-pink peonies and pale pink Oriental poppies in Monet's garden

Papaver rhoeas (SHIRLEY POPPY, CORN POPPY)

This hardy annual grows wild throughout the temperate Old World, especially in pastureland that was cultivated the previous year and then left fallow. The fields and orchards sparkling with red poppies are among the best-known Impressionist images. Cassatt, Hassam, Monet, Renoir and Van Gogh were all drawn to the brilliant, iridescent qualities of the fragile flowers. Monet sprinkled them through the beds in his flower garden to add a touch of informality, while Renoir let them naturalize in his olive orchard. The saucer-shaped flowers of Shirley poppies grow up to 10 cm (4 in) across. Though the Impressionists painted mostly the scarlet kind, colors today include white, pink, reddish-orange, and lavender – some with black or white markings at the base of each petal. They resent transplanting, but grow quickly from seed sown onto the surface of bare soil, and will tolerate mild frosts. Though not long-lasting as cut flowers, unless the cut ends are seared with boiling water or a hot iron, Van Gogh showed them massed in a vase in several canvases. Celia Thaxter also treasured them as cut flowers, and Hassam painted her study full of arrangements of red corn poppies mixed with yellow and orange Iceland poppies *(P. nudicaule)*.

Trailing ivy-leaved geraniums in Renoir's garden

Pelargonium (BEDDING GERANIUM)

Today, many gardeners scoff at the idea of using bedding geraniums in a garden because they are so common. They were also common during the Impressionist era – popular in parks and gardens everywhere – yet the Impressionists planted them and painted them, mostly for their rich green leaves and clean reds – factors that Renoir used to advantage in his painting *Flowers and Cats* (1881). Monet, Caillebotte, Pissarro, Cézanne and Manet also painted displays of geraniums in pots. Cézanne often showed them with no flowers at all – just contorted bare stems with a topknot of ruffled leaves, against a sunny wall of his studio. Pots of geraniums are grown in Cézanne's garden today, while at the entrance to Renoir's house tall terracotta

urns overflow with the pink and red ivy-leaved kind. Often grown – then as now – as annuals for their summer-long color, pelargoniums are tender perennials and are native to South Africa. Their immense popularity in the Impressionist era was made possible by the development, at the time, of commercial greenhouses where they could be cultivated in enormous numbers. They were usually massed, in patterns with other colorful annuals such as verbena or lobelia, in geometric-shaped beds set into green lawns. Monet's many paintings of his houses at Vétheuil and Argenteuil, and Caillebotte's of his family home at Yerres show these kind of formal beds heaped with color. While Monet abandoned the smooth grass as a backdrop to his beds at Giverny, he used zonal pelargoniums as bedding in the formal island beds on the terrace immediately in front of his house. The Regal geranium is grown mostly as a pot plant. The ivy-leaved geranium is best used as a cascading plant, tumbling from window boxes and spilling over retaining walls, though it can be trained to scramble up a trellis. Geraniums tolerate periods of drought, and require twelve hours of daylight for good flowering though the Regal and ivy-leaved kinds bloom best when nights are cool. They are all propagated easily from cuttings. Some bedding geraniums grow from seed and generally produce a longer-lasting display than those grown from cuttings.

Prunus (ALMOND, APRICOT, CHERRY, PEACH, PLUM)

Native to Asia, these early-flowering trees were painted in Normandy by Monet and Pissarro, and in the south of France by Van Gogh. Apple and pear trees were also a popular subject of Sisley and many American Impressionists. There are lots of fruit trees today in Monet's flower garden – espaliered apples and pears, fastigiate cherries, and weeping crab apples among others – where they provide strong vertical accents and dappled shade as well as airy clouds of spring colors. Such trees require full sun, fertile, well drained soil, and pruning to maintain an open arrangement of branches for good air circulation to encourage abundant fruiting. A single branch of blossom can make a dramatic indoor arrangement, as shown in Van Gogh's several paintings of almond branches in glass vases.

Van Gogh Pink Peach Trees *(1888)*

Rosa (ROSE)

The Hybrid Tea rose came into cultivation during the Impressionist era. Developed by a French rose breeder, the first was named 'La France'. It is a large, high-centerd pink rose with a pleasant fragrance reminiscent of tea leaves. However, the Impressionists grew and painted what are now considered old-fashioned roses – particularly those with cupped flowers and a tight petal arrangement, and with a heavy, fruity fragrance. Monet planted roses extensively in his Giverny garden, using them in all shapes and sizes – shrub roses, Floribundas, standard roses and climbers. 'Belle Vichysoise', a vigorous climber, was one of his favorites; at Giverny dense clusters of its small pink double flowers cascade down a high arbor over the boat dock in the water garden. To form a canopy over the porch of his house, Monet grew another vigorous climber 'Mermaid' – a saucer-shaped, single creamy-yellow rose with an amber crown of powdery stamens at the center of each fragrant flower, and with black-green glossy foliage. Other climbers today that are trained over the metal arches of his Grande Allée display colors that range from the brilliant red of 'Paul's Scarlet Climber' to the silvery-pink of 'New Dawn' and clear yellow of 'Golden Showers'. One of Renoir's favorite roses was 'Painter Renoir', which was named after him and still grows in the garden at Les Collettes. A pale pink shrub rose with several layers

Rosa *'Belle Vichysoise' in Monet's garden*

Detail from Renoir Vase of Moss Roses *(1866)*

of petals forming a cup-shaped bloom up to 10 cm (4 in) across, it grows a dense mass of arching canes that can be trained to climb but also look stunning trailing down a dry bank or wall. Finding roses that would have been grown at the turn of the century is not difficult as many reputable suppliers list the date of introduction. If they were alive today the Impressionists would have welcomed the new English roses bred in Great Britain by David Austin, as these resilient, repeat-flowering roses are reminiscent in shape and smell of old-fashioned varieties that generally bloom only once each year. Roses do best in a sunny location and prefer fertile, well-drained, humus-rich soil. Although Hybrid Tea roses survive longest as cut flowers (especially if cut in the "mature-bud" stage), the older varieties respond well to having their stems crushed just before they are put in water.

Syringa vulgaris (LILAC)

Native to Europe and Asia, these hardy deciduous shrubs bear very fragrant flower clusters that are most usually mauve or pink, but can also be purple-blue or white. The Impressionists painted them in public parks, private gardens and the cut flowers as still lifes, often as part of an informal flower arrangement. Monet's *The Lilac Bower* (see page 74), of which there are several versions, shows people seated under an arching canopy of flowering lilac branches. New lilac cultivars are especially beautiful and are a feature of Monet's garden today. Three of the best are 'Madame Lemoine' (pure white), 'Maréchal Lannes' (deep violet) and 'Président Grévy' (powder-blue). Lilacs are easy to grow, preferring full sun and an alkaline, well drained soil. Brought inside, the flowers will soon fill a room with their heady scent.

Cassatt Lilacs in a Window *(c. 1889)*

Tulipa (TULIP)

Monet used tulips throughout his flower garden, planting them in the island beds near the house, in clumps in the grass, and in ribbons in his long narrow beds. He chose them, as gardeners do today, not only for a huge variety in color but also for the successive blooming from early single tulips through to late lily-flowered kinds. Tulips appear in still lifes by Monet and Renoir, and Monet chose the tulip fields of Holland for a series of paintings sponsored by a Dutch diplomat. Tulips are hardy bulbs and come in a color range that is one of the richest in horticulture, from white to a near-black with all shades between except for a true blue. In the garden, tulips are invaluable for an early splash of bright color, and Monet used bi-colored tulips to add a sparkle to his garden in the spring. Since Monet's day, many improvements in size have been made to tulips – particularly the Darwin hybrids, and there are many new large doubles, such as the double late (peony-flowered) group. However, the floral display of the Darwin hybrids is short-lived compared to the old-fashioned singles (and the petals shatter easily in rain); and Monet would probably have shunned double-flowered tulips as he generally preferred single petalled flowers. Tulips do best in well-drained soil, where they can get a summer baking. In cool, wet areas, the bulbs are best lifted after the leaves have died down, and stored in a dry place for replanting in the autumn.

'Greenland' and 'White Triumphator' tulips among blue forget-me-nots, gold and bronze wallflowers and black and white pansies in Monet's garden.

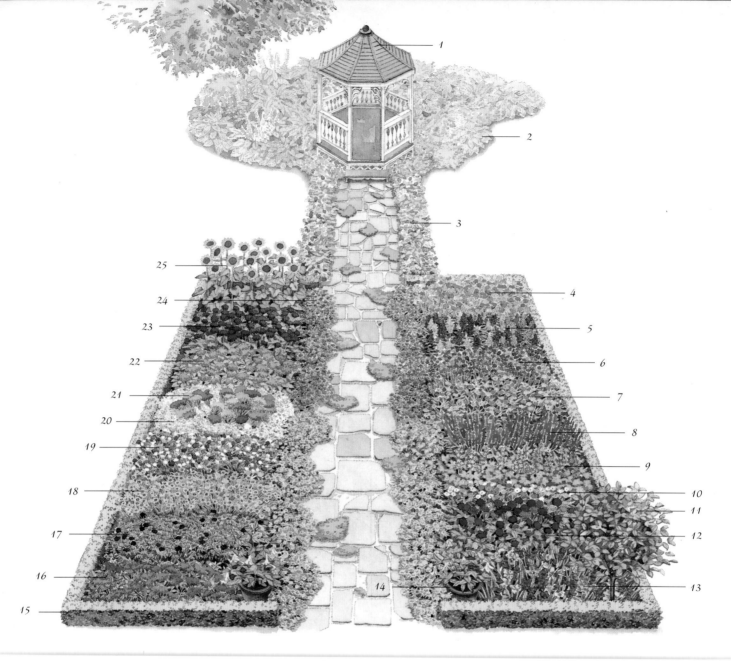

CEDARIDGE FARM CUTTING GARDEN
Based on Van Gogh's painting of a
farmer's cutting garden, Flower
Garden with Path *(see page 2), this*
garden was winner of the 1991
Homestyle Garden Design Contest for
a successful interpretation of an
Impressionist garden and received an
award from the Pennsylvania
Horticultural Society for Best Flower
Garden in their 1993 Garden Design
Contest. Here it is seen in
mid-summer.

1   *Gazebo*
2   *Shade garden*
3   *Tuberous begonia 'Nonstop'*
4   Cosmos *'Sensation'*
5   Antirrhinum majus
6   Centaurea cyanus
7   Calendula officinalis *Pacific mixed*
8   Salvia farinacea *'Victoria'*
9   Consolida ambigua *'Imperial Blue'*
10 Papaver rhoeas
11 Syringa vulgaris
12 *Pompon dahlias*

13 Gladiolus
14 Datura *(in pots)*
15 *Box hedging*
16 Heliotrope *'Marine'*
17 Scabiosa atropurpurea
18 Gomphrena globosa
19 Coreopsis tinctoria
20 Gypsophila elegans
21 Callistephus
22 Celosia *'Apricot Beauty'*
23 Zinnia *'Cherry Ruffles'*
24 Tagetes patula
25 Helianthus annuus

138

Places to Visit

FRANCE
Cézanne's Garden and Studio
Avenue Paul Cézanne
13090 Aix-en-Provence
Tel: 42 21 06 53

Musée Marmottan,
2, rue Louis Boilly, 75016 Paris
Tel: 42 24 07 02
(Large exhibit of Monet's art and artefacts)

Musée Americain Giverny
Rue Claude Monet, 27620 Giverny
Tel: 32 51 94 65
(Exhibition of American Impressionist Art)

Musée Claude Monet
Rue Claude Monet, 27620 Giverny
Tel: 32 51 28 21

Musée de Montmartre
12, rue Cortot, 75018 Paris
Tel: 46 06 61 11
(Residence once occupied by Renoir)

Musée d'Orsay
62, rue de Lille, 75007 Paris
Tel: 40 49 48 14
(Contains all the Impressionist paintings
formerly in the Louvre Museum)

Orangerie des Tuileries
Place de la Concorde, 74001 Paris
Tel: 42 97 48 16
(Houses Monet's waterlily panels)

Parc de Caillebotte
6, rue de Coney, 91330 Yerres

Renoir Museum and Garden
Chemin des Collettes
06800 Cagnes-sur-Mer
Tel: 93 20 61 07

Van Gogh's Walk, Arles
In the Place du Forum, 13200 Arles,
Provence, gift shops sell *Arles Van Gogh*,
by C. Wentinck and L.Clergue, with
maps that show the location of many
Van Gogh motifs

Van Gogh's Walk, Auvers-sur-Oise
Contact The Tourist Office,
Manoir des Colombières
Rue Sansonne, 95430 Auvers-Sur-Oise
Tel: 30 26 10 06

Van Gogh's Walk, Saint-Rémy
Contact The Office of Tourism, Place
Jaures, 13210 Saint-Rémy-de-Provence
Tel: 90 92 05 22

HOLLAND
Kröller-Müller Museum
Apeldoornseweg No 250
7351 TA, Otterlo
Tel: 08382 1041
(Large collection of Van Gogh's work)

Vincent Van Gogh National Museum
Stadhouderskade No 42
1071 ZD Amsterdam
Tel: 020 67 32 121

UNITED STATES
The Barnes Foundation
300 N Latch's Lane
Merion Station, PA 19066
Tel: 215 667 0290
(Major collection of Impressionist Art)

Celia Thaxter Garden
Appledore Island,
Isle of Shoals, Maine
Tel: (Shoals Marine Laboratory)
607 255 3717

Cedaridge Farm
Box 1, Gardenville, PA 18926
Tel: 215 766 0699
Visits by appointment only

Further Reading

Patrick Bade, *Renoir - The Masterworks*, 1989, Portland House
Judith Bumpus, *Impressionist Gardens*, 1990, Phaidon Press
Judith Bumpus, *Van Gogh's Flowers*, 1989, Universe Books
Jean-Paul Crespelle, *Guide de la France Impressioniste*, Sites, Musées, Promenades, 1990, Les Guides Visuels, Hazan
Barbara Ehrlich White, *Renoir – His Life, Art and Letters*, 1984, Harry N. Abrams Inc
William Feaver, *Van Gogh – The Masterworks*, 1990, Portland House
Amy Fine Collins, *American Impressionism*, 1990, Brampton Books Corp
Robert Gordon and Andrew Forge, *Monet*, 1983, Harry N. Abrams Inc
Claire Joyes, *Claude Monet – Life at Giverny*, 1985, Vendome Press
Metropolitan Museum of Art, *Monet's Years at Giverny: beyond Impressionism*, 1978

Museum of Fine Arts, Boston, *Renoir*, 1985
David Park Curry, *Childe Hassam – An Island Garden Revisited*, 1990, Denver Art Museum/ WW Norton & Co Inc
Gilles Plazy, *Cézanne*, 1990, Crescent Books
Jay Roudebush, *Cassatt*, 1979, Bonfini Press Corp
Belinda Thompson and Michael Howard, *Impressionism*, 1988, Exeter Books
Ambroise Vollard, *Cézanne*, 1984, Dover Publications
Ingo F. Walther and Rainer Metzer, *Vincent Van Gogh – The Complete Paintings*, Vol II, 1990, Benridkt Taschen Verlag GmbH & Co
Pierre Wittmer, *Caillebotte And His Garden at Yerres*, (1991), Harry N. Abrams Inc
— *Pissarro*, 1990, Phidal; 1988, Gruppo Editoriale Fabbri SpA
— *Sisley*, 1990, Phidal; 1988, Gruppo Editoriale Fabbri SpA

Index

AUTHOR'S ACKNOWLEDGMENTS

In a book of this scope, a lifetime of friendships and associations - with gardeners, writers, teachers of art history, artists themselves and other photographers - help to produce the end result, too many to include the names of everyone.

However, I single out my friend, Hiroshi Makita, a talented garden designer, who taught me about Japanese garden art through a tour of his gardens in the USA, and during a visit we made together to the Imperial gardens of Kyoto, Japan, in 1990.

I value the support of my wife, Carolyn, who in 1990 and 1992 accompanied me to many of the Impressionist gardens featured in this book, and Kathy Nelson, my administrative assistant, Wendy Fields, my grounds supervisor, and David Sike, who designed and constructed many of the Impressionist structures featured at my home, Cedaridge Farm.

Thanks also to Jacques Renoir, great-grandson of the painter, whom I met during a photography assignment for the Cote d'Azur Office of Tourism in 1989. Jacques and his friend, Michel Colas (who at the time worked for the Office of Tourism), both helped me research the life of Renoir and understand Renoir's garden philosophy, which is described more fully in my book *Renoir's Garden*, (1991, Frances Lincoln Ltd).

I must also mention Olive Dunn, a talented garden colorist, whose inspirational Impressionist-like garden I photographed at Invercargill, New Zealand, in 1993.

Finally, a word of appreciation for the staff at Frances Lincoln Ltd, who brought to the work a wealth of good insights and ideas; plus thanks to Liz Pepperell who took my scribbled rough layouts and rendered them so beautifully.   *D.F.*

PUBLISHERS' ACKNOWLEDGMENTS

The publishers would like to thank Liz Pepperell for the artwork, Tony Lord for horticultural advice, Helen Baz for the index, Sue Gladstone for the picture research, and Adela Cory for her help with the production.

PHOTOGRAPHIC ACKNOWLEDGMENTS

Please note that many of the paintings reproduced in this book are not shown in their entirety. The Publishers have made every effort to contact all holders of copyright works. All copyright-holders we have been unable to reach are invited to contact the Publishers so that a full acknowledgment may be given in subsequent editions. For permission to reproduce the paintings and photographs and for supplying photographs, the Publishers thank those listed below.

(L=left R=right A=above B=below): Ader-Tajan, Paris 120; The Art Institute of Chicago (photographs © 1993) 68,78L,106; Collection Beyeler, Basle 104; Brame & Lorenceau 5,128; The Bridgeman Art Library 7,30,44,96 (Giraudon),111 (courtesy of Fitzwilliam Museum, University of Cambridge),112-13,114 (courtesy of Smithsonian Institute/Art Resource),121 (Giraudon), 131 (Lauros-Giraudon); The Carnegie Museum of Art

ABOVE *The surface of the pond at Giverny is cleared regularly so that there is enough space between the waterlily islands to show reflections on the water.*

(acquired through the generosity of Mrs. Alan M.Scaife, 65.35) 126; Cincinnatti Art Museum (bequest of Mary E. Johnston) 100; Durand-Ruel, Paris 22L; The Fogg Art Museum (bequest of Grenville L. Winthrop) 132; Foundation E.G. Bührle Collection 54L; Haags Gemeentemuseum, The Hague 3; Hirschl & Adler Galleries, Inc 36; Yves Jannès (courtesy Editions d'art Monelle Hayot) 32-3; Kröller-Müller State Museum, Otterlo, The Netherlands 102,134; Andrew Lawson 45,57, 68-9,73,80-1,84A,93,100,102-3,116; The Metropolitan Museum of Art 76; Achim Moeller Fine Art, New York (John C.Whitehead Collection) 78R; Musée d'Orsay 11,27 (© photo R.M.N.), 28 (© photo R.M.N.), 74 (© photo R.M.N.),118,135; Musée Marmottan 46-47,54-5,55R,86,125; The Museum of Fine Arts, Houston (The John A. and Audrey Jones Beck Collection) 10; The Museum of Modern Art, New York 60 (gift of Sylvia Slifka in memory of Joseph Slifka), 116 (photo Nickolas Muray); National Academy of Design, New York 124; The Nelson-Atkins Museum of Art, Kansas City, Missouri (purchase Nelson Trust, 32-2) 98; Österreichische Galerie, Vienna 12; Shelley Rotner 114-15; SYGMA 15; Terra Museum of American Art, Chicago (Daniel J. Terra Collection, 37.1986) 130; Thyssen-Bornemisza Collection 92; Vincent van Gogh Foundation/Van Gogh Museum, Amsterdam 79,103,127; Wadsworth Atheneaum, Hartford (bequest of Anne Parrish Titzell) 8,122; Yale University Art Gallery (gift of Mr and Mrs Paul Mellon, B.A.1929) 40